# Seeds for
# Enlightenment
# 101

## JoAnn James

ISBN 978-1-63961-321-2 (paperback)
ISBN 978-1-63961-322-9 (digital)

Christian Faith Publishing, Inc.
832 Park Avenue
Meadville, PA 16335
www.christianfaithpublishing.com

Printed in the United States of America

# One Hundred Days of Happy

*I*t seems that every week a new movement surfaces. Lately there has been a diverse selection of hash tags. Most of these movements involve other people.

The "random acts of kindness" movement, where a person unselfishly and spontaneously volunteers to show kindness to someone helps both the receiver and the giver. The recipient of this kind act could be a family member, someone in your church family, a friend, a neighbor, or an absolute stranger. The deed might be paying the turnpike toll for the car following behind you, cutting your neighbor's lawn when you do your mowing, or when dining out, have the server bring you the tab for a nearby table. It is amazing how a small gesture of kindness affects people and helps ease burdens. Personally, I have tried this practice and the results are tremendous.

The "pay it forward" movement also provides an opportunity to share your blessings and let someone know that there are still people who care.

Both movements require action and provide an opportunity to show agape love, which bring to mind part of a poem that says, "The love in your heart was not put there to stay. Love isn't love until it is given away." Isn't that true of blessings also?

While sharing is important, taking care of oneself is critical! Whenever you board a ship, one of the first things you must do is attend a safety meeting. The staff gives directions on where the lifesaving equipment is located, how to use the lifesaving vests, and how to disembark the vessel. The same type of safety procedures is protocol when on an airplane. Simple fact is, you must take care of yourself if want to be able to take care of or help others. If you happen to be a caregiver, you need to be aware of and take advantage of respite services. Take a break and recoup before you wear out.

All of this brings me to the "one hundred days of happy" movement—taking care of you! Get a journal, small notebook, smart phone—whatever—and begin to log. The intent is to find something, each day, for the next one hundred days, that makes you happy, and record it in your journal. The purpose being that after one hundred days, you will have formed a "good "positive habit that leads to healthy, happy, enjoyable living. My one hundred days of happy began with seeing two huge red blossoms on the amaryllis in my sunroom. Such beauty provides yet another opportunity to thank God for all His creations. Instead of thinking about or worrying about problems, look for positive things. Your happy will be different from my happy, but identifying your happy will lead to healthier, happier living. It will help you forget about pain and problems and cause you look to the future with hope. Moreover, like the words to one of my favorite songs, "It only takes a spark to get a fire going…" I encourage you to try one hundred days of happy and rediscover happiness, one day at a time!

"Though outwardly we are wasting away, yet inwardly we are being renewed day by day" (2 Corinthians 4:16 NIV).

# A Season for Everything

*C*hange is inevitable and things truly do not stay the same. It is amazing how the same word can cause different reactions and thoughts, depending on where you are in life and what you may be doing, or what may be occurring in your immediate surroundings. Ecclesiastes 3:1 tells us, "There is a time for *everything* and a season for *every* activity under heaven," and it even goes on to give a list of related positive and negative activities as examples. Yet every time I visit this scripture, different fleeting thoughts invade my mind. The words everything and every pop out so profoundly right now. Not some things, not a few things, BUT everything!

Between birth and death, we all experience a variety of events and life changes—some simple and many that are complex.

How do we handle the complex situations that arise in our lives? Have we learned how to peacefully survive trials and tribulations? Do we rely on the promises, knowing that "this too will pass?"

One of my favorite scriptures is found in Isaiah 40:28–31. It serves as a reminder of how great our God is and how awesome He is in taking care of us through any storm.

Knowing that God is in control of our lives, making "everything beautiful in its times," brings, comfort, peace, and hope.

Being a little "under the weather," I was recently blessed to have my daughter be my caregiver for a few days. This reverse role stirred up thoughts and admittedly a little anxiety, about changing images of a mother and how these images unfold:

Four-year-old: "My mommy can do anything!"
Eight-year-old: "My mom knows a lot! A whole lot!"

Twelve-year-old: "My mother doesn't really know quite everything."
Fourteen-year-old: "Naturally, Mom doesn't know that either."
Sixteen-year-old: "Mom? She's hopelessly old-fashioned."
Eighteen-year-old: "That old woman? She's way out of date!"
Twenty-five-year-old: "Well, she might know a little bit about it."
Thirty-year-old: "She's smarter that she used to be."
Thirty-five-year-old: "Before we decide, let's get Mom's opinion."
Fifty-year-old: "Wonder what Mom would have thought about it?"
Sixty-five-year-old: "Wish I could talk it over with Mom."

I am counting my blessings! Truly, there is a season for EVERYTHING!

"There is a time for everything, and a season for every activity under heaven" (Ecclesiastes 3:1).

# A Brand-New Year

*W*ow! It is here—January: the beginning a brand-new year. "The old has gone, the new is here" (2 Corinthians 5:17).

The month of January is named after the Roman god *Janus* who is depicted with two faces. One face is looking into the past, and the other is looking to the future.

Wouldn't it be great if we put the past behind us—especially the negative—and look to the future with hope? It all begins with a mindset that hopefully will lead to a change of heart.

I begin my day with a poem penned by Helen Steiner Rice. It reads like this:

> Good Morning God, you are ushering in another day untouched and freshly new, so here I come to ask You, God, if You will renew me too? Forgive the many errors that I made yesterday, and let me try again, dear God, to walk closer in Thy way. But Father, I am aware I cannot make it on my own, so take my hand and hold it tight for I cannot walk alone.

I should have it memorized, but I do not. It is comforting to hold it and read it, as it gives perspective to my daily walk.

Moving into a new year and cleaning out the old, I cling to a large outdated calendar. This calendar, a gift from my niece, is titled "Words to live by." It is an eighteen-month calendar, and each month shares a gem of wisdom to guide you on a journey to live each day to the fullest, and to appreciate the gifts already in your possession.

I am going to share some of those sayings—with my added perspective, of course!

**Believe in your Selfie.** While our culture fixates on outward appearances, know that our Heavenly Father sees things quite differently. The selfie should remind you that you are God's uniquely created person. "The Lord delights in you" (Isaiah 62:4). That selfie is like looking in the mirror. It is a reminder and confirmation that "I am fearfully and wonderfully made" (1 Corinthians 13:12).

**Be so happy that when others look at you, they become happy too.** We know that a smile is contagious and is recognized in any language. Smile often! "A happy heart makes the face cheerful" (Proverbs 15:13).

**An attitude of gratitude brings great things:** "Thanks be to God! He gives us the victory through our Lord Jesus Christ" (1 Corinthians 15:57). Tack onto that Psalms 100.

**Be strong you never know who you are inspiring.** "Stand firm, let nothing move you. Always give yourself fully to the work of the Lord..." (1 Corinthians 15:58).

**I see no good reason to act my age.** (One of my favorites!) "He crowns you with love and compassion and so satisfies your desires with good things so that your youth is renewed" (Psalms 103:4–5). That is my story, and I'm sticking to it!

**You can never have too much happy.** "Ask and you will receive, and your joy will be complete" (John 16:24). "May the God of hope fill you with all joy and peace as you trust in him, so that you may overflow with hope by the power of the Holy Spirit" (Romans 15:3).

**Accept the fact that some days you are the pigeon, and some days you are the statue.** "He makes his sun rise on the evil and the good, and sends rain on the just and unjust..." (Matthew 5:45). "Give thanks in all circumstances" (1 Thessalonians 5:17). This is not an easy one!

**The first step to getting what you want is having the courage to get rid of what you don't.** This one speaks to me in two different veins. "For God did not give us a spirit of timidity, but a spirit of power, love and self-discipline" (2 Timothy 1:7). "I tell you the truth, unless a kernel of wheat falls to the ground and dies, it remains only a single seed, but if it dies, it produces many seeds" (John 12:12). You gotta get rid of the old, to have space for the new.

Are you ready and willing to usher in a New Year with a brand-new attitude?

# A Hearty Appetite

With obesity being so common, it is not hard to believe that many among us have a hearty appetite for food. Food choices do determine what happens to our bodies—both internally and externally. Therefore, we must learn to control our appetites for certain foods and for overeating. Controlling a hearty appetite for food can be a challenge.

Hunger pangs are good things. They teach us to appreciate our appetite for food and indicate you are alive, have feeling, and are healthy. Satisfy those pangs and you are good to go!

Illness and/or certain medications may cause us to lose our appetite. I hope that this is temporary. Even though you need nourishment to recover, food may not be appealing, nothing tastes good, or you just may not want to eat. These are the times when we may wish for a hearty appetite. These are the times when we realize that a hearty appetite for food is a good friend—a gift from God to heal and protect us. Proverbs 27:7 tells us, "When you are full, you will refuse honey, but when you are hungry even bitter food tastes sweet."

Another appetite may be for music. Think about taking a long trip and driving without any music in the background. For some (like me) this may be peaceful. For those with a hearty appetite for music or noise, the trip would almost be unbearable.

Then there are those who have a desire to sport the latest fashions and always be in style. They have a hearty appetite for clothes and fashion.

Then there are many who have a hearty appetite for the Word. They read. They study. They pray. They digest the Word and can share and discuss the Word. When they pray, they also listen. Then they apply what He says—the Word—to their life, and in service to others. There is a sincere connection and relationship with our Savior. This comes from having a hearty appetite for the Word! This appetite will not lead to the problem of obesity or affect your external appearance, but it will change what is happening on the inside. Your heart and mind will be renewed—like wow! "Blessed are those who hunger and thirst for righteousness, for they shall be filled" (Matthew 5:6).

"Blessed are you who hunger now, for you will be satisfied" (Luke 6:21).

Take a few minutes and read Psalm 107 and you will see how a hearty appetite for the Word will satisfy **ALL** your needs!

# A Holy Connection

*W*e have come this far by faith…

Early in the seventies, the YWCA focused on the "Elimination of Racism." During that time, I was a board member and participated in many panel discussions on this topic. I am saddened to say, racism still exists. I do not believe America will ever be fair to all its people.

February is designated as Black History Month. During this month, many organizations and some churches set up displays, offer programs, and attempt to call attention to, or recognize contributions to our society by Black Americans.

In the sixties, Blacks/African Americans began to collectively move forward, and toward openly loving ourselves. We began to proudly embrace our hair, our color, and our features. Doing such made us stronger. The problem is that the growth period and the moments of self-love did not continue and did not go deep enough. It was almost like a new Christian, starting on milk and never progressing to meat.

The sixties was like an Rx. There was a strong movement toward equality and eliminating racism, but it is as if we did not take the medicine long enough for the healing to take place. Was the prescription not strong enough? Was it like many of the medicines and drugs of today—too expensive for our pockets or too cost-prohibitive for our lives? Did the marching, sitting in, and trying to integrate, overshadow the ability to learn to love self and value what God endowed us with and bestowed upon us?

I do not expect racism to ever disappear. So what do we do? We must learn to respond to racism in a self-affirming and not self-defeating way. Self-affirmation is internal and begins with learning to love yourself. Believing in your dreams and aspirations. "For thou has possessed my reins; thou hast covered me in my mother's womb. I will praise thee; for I am wonderfully made; marvelous are thy works; and that my soul knoweth right well" (Psalm 139:13–14). You are special and God loves you.

The challenge we African Americans face today is to throw off the stigma of imposed slavery, racism, and injustice and to explore the liberation of being enslaved, by our own choice, to God (salvation). Choosing salvation, gives us the power and the gifts we need to live a joyous, peaceful, and prosperous life (Romans 8:22–23).

In American society, some believe that African Americans could never contribute or amount to anything, but out of a people connected with God's grace came educator Booker T. Washington, scientist George Washington Carver, activist Fannie Lou Hamer, astronaut Ron McNair, singer Marian Andersen, and Chairman of the Joint Chief of Staff General Colin Powell—to name just a few. We should also not forget Henrietta Lacks and the travesty of her life and contribution.

Paul's letter to the Ephesian church discusses the connection our society needs—a holy connection (Ephesians 2:4–5).

Paul also reminds us that where divisions once existed, Jesus has broken down the barriers. His teachings give us hope for a reconciled society. The joy is that it begins in you and in me. When we start a loving relationship with our self, we are able, through Jesus Christ, to do away with hatred and suspicion toward one another, and live together in peace and harmony. "For through him we both have access by one spirit to the Father" (Ephesians 2:18).

That is the holy connection.

# Will a Little Dab Do Ya'?

*S*ome commercials have been memorialized and will remain a part of advertising history. While jingles or phrases are specifically meant for one product, the catchy phrases are often applied to other things or situations. Many of you may remember Brylcreem's claim that "a little dab'll do you." Personally, I have never tried it, so I am unable to vouch for the product, but I have used the phrase many times, in other situations.

Very similarly, Maxwell House coffee claims, "Good to the last drop." Is it? These memorable phrases are sometimes used in playing games at parties and showers, and it is fun to see how many folks recall these advertisements. It is even more interesting to see how often these phrases are used to relate to other things.

With Brylcreem, a little dab might do it; a little dab will not work for your Christian walk. James 1:22 (NIV) tells us, "Do not merely listen to the Word and so deceive yourselves. Do what it says."

Easter, Christmas, and Mother's Day visits to church are dabs, and certainly will not enhance your opportunity to establish a connection and meaningful relationship with God. We know that actions do not give us salvation, but our actions are a good indicator of whether you are truly saved. Think about the woman with the alabaster box. She gave mightily—using all the expensive oil she carried in the alabaster box—to anoint Jesus, not just a little dab. How many of us would have used a little dab? When I have an expensive bottle of perfume, especially one that I really like, I am very careful to use a little dab at a time—making it last if possible. Not only that, but no one could also come too close to me if I used the whole bottle at once! In this instance, a little dab does do it!

How often do we claim we would give our all for God, knowing that we would only give a controlled portion? We need to focus on giving our attention, our gifts, our talents, and our thoughts to God. Remember our Christian walk is not like Brylcreem. A little here and there will not cut it! A little church, a little prayer, a little study, a little giving, or a little faith does not follow the alleged claim of a little dab of Brylcreem! Go for the gusto! Look for ways to be open and use more than just a little dab. Increase your acts of faithfulness by giving your time, talents, and treasures; studying to show thyself approved; praying and talking with God; listening for His direction; and finally, yet importantly connecting with a church. Remember, there is a fullness of life that can only be found in Jesus Christ.

# A Three-Day Affair

$\mathcal{S}$ ounds kinda sleazy and sinful, doesn't it? On the other hand, maybe just a little provocative and enticing! Well, now that I have your attention, I will tell you the "real deal"!

Each year, the weekend after Labor Day, the West Virginia Black Heritage Festival (WVBHF) convenes in downtown Clarksburg. While this festival commemorates history and the struggles and advancements of African Americans, we promote and embrace diversity. These three days are devoted to families reuniting—biological families, church families, school mates, neighborhood buddies, etc. It is a time for a food fest—you can indulge in foods of all ethnic groups—especially "soul food": sweet potato pie, fried fish, ribs and Marino Brothers' sandwiches, to name a few. It is a wonderful opportunity to greet, meet, and share with many different people, renew some old friendships, and possibly make some new friends. The vendors from the tri-state area make shopping interesting—displaying jewelry, art, clothing, books, and even free health screenings.

Friday evening is devoted to our Youth. Approximately 150 to 200 youth enjoy a block party, featuring a live DJ, dancing, games, and FREE food. This fun-filled event is co-sponsored by Pierpont Community & Technical College, Fairmont State University, McDonald's, and Fresh Express.

During the opening ceremony on Saturday, the king and queen will be crowned. After this, the real festivities begin—live music, food, and vendor booths. There is something for everyone! The family-oriented atmosphere provides a safe, fun-filled day with lots of pleasant memories.

Sunday is here and you are in for a real treat—a gospel explosion! The wide genre and variety of music and spirit-filled musicians provide you an experience you can't imagine. You must be there to see for yourself. If you have attended the WVBHF in the past, you are aware of the uniqueness. If you have not attended before, try it. You might really like it! Talking about just a three-day affair—but be careful, you could possibly be hooked! "Your statutes are my heritage forever; they are joy in my heart" (Psalms 119:111).

# A Winning Attitude

*I*n an effort to be better organized, right size, and get rid of clutter in 2016, my daughter and I began a "cleaning up and clearing out" project. Believe me, this is a very difficult and time-consuming task. Moreover, it is so interesting to see what things have been saved over the years, and it is very hard to part with some of the items that have been very meaningful and treasured at some time. However, we did it! Mission accomplished—at least phase one!

One of my found "saves" is a 1994 West Virginia University Extension Service article authored by Patricia R. Gruber and Shirley C. Eagan, titled "The Winning Attitude." The thoughts and words in this article are timeless and still apply today.

A portion of the article is as follows:

> Life is like a journey at sea. Some days are peaceful, with sunlit blue skies, calm waters, and gentle breezes filling our sails. Many days present us an abundance of interesting and often unexpected challenges. At times, high waves crash all around and the sky darkens as heavy storms approach. Whatever experiences come along; you'll navigate them more carefully if you master your attitude. Doing so will not make your problems go away. It will, however, make your journey more enjoyable and rewarding. You will experience greater understanding, enthusiasm, and endurance. You'll find yourself "breezin'

through life," embracing the lessons and opportunities that come your way.

Life is not always a bed of roses. Things happening, and the people around us can and often do cause turmoil. The above quote is a reminder of the promise, "I will be with you; I will never leave you or forsake you" (Joshua 1:5). That is our relief and release!

The article goes on to say:

> Whatever experiences come along; you'll navigate them more skillfully if you master your attitude. Doing so will not make your problems go away. It will, however, make your journey more enjoyable and rewarding. You will experience greater understanding, enthusiasm, and endurance. You'll find yourself "breezin' through life," embracing the lessons and opportunities that come your way.

Maintaining or striving to maintain a positive attitude helps overcome so many obstacles. It also keeps you healthy and happy. Learning to be thankful for what you have, instead of worrying and fretting about what you don't have will put a smile on your face and release the tension and stress you may be harboring. An attitude of gratitude goes a mighty long way! Your attitude is one of the things in life that you can control and change. Let your choice be a winning positive attitude!

Some thoughts to keep in mind as you choose to make your attitude, one of gratitude:

- The eyes shout what the lips fear to say.
- Whatever we gain each year is not to be a level on which we stop but a plateau on which we ascend.
- Happiness comes through doors you did not know you left open.

- Do not cry because it's over; smile because it happened.
- You cannot make footprints in the sands of time sitting down.

Each morning when you arise, give thanks for one more day. Anticipate with enthusiasm what positive choices you will make, and let the Son shine in. You will be blessed! Wishing you a "too blessed to be stressed "attitude in this year and all those that follow.

# AKA

*A*KA—*also known as*! This may or may not be a familiar acronym to you; however, it is a practice that is commonly used. Many times, AKAs are unintentional, but often they may be intentional. For instance, someone may use their initials followed by their last name, or they may use a first name, middle initial, and last name, or they may use just a first and last name. When this happens, the credit reports may list all the variations as AKA. Usually, this is not a problem. Sometimes it just happens because you are rushing to sign your name or fill out an application, and usually there is no malevolence.

When a business entity does this, what is the intent? Why does this happen? There possibly could be many reasons, some legitimate and others devious.

Consumers should be aware that there are some unscrupulous businesses that have several AKAs, and they change their business name as often as the law allows. This is their way of evading unsatisfied customers, not fulfilling promises, not completing projects, and reneging on warranties.

A few years ago, I contracted for a major home remodeling project. I did not do my research and made a poor choice for a contractor. Months after the project was complete, there was noticeable warping and discoloration of the materials that came with a lifetime warranty. Upon contacting the company, I was advised that a representative would visit and assess the problem. The representative did visit, take pictures, measurements, and advise that he would schedule a work crew to correct the problem. This did not happen. Follow-up calls made it clear that the telephone number on the contract was no longer in service, and there was no longer any listing for Company X.

Subsequently, I began receiving marketing calls from Company Y for home remodeling services. Curiosity led me to ask the names of the company owners. Turned out, the owners of Company Y were the same names on my contract with Company X. This led me to contact the Better Business Bureau. I learned that Company Y had the same physical address and the same proprietors listed as did Company X. Not only that, there were also other prior business listings under the same owners names and at that same address. The difference being the name of the business and the telephone number. History confirmed that approximately every three years there was a business name change.

I contacted the company with this newfound information. Of course, they denied any relation or connection to Company X. At this point, I knew I was a victim.

Nevertheless, God's way of working in mysterious ways became apparent.

A few weeks later, I received a random marketing call for home improvement opportunities. This provided an opportunity to sched-ule an appointment with Company Y. I scheduled the appointment just to have a face-to-face contact with a company representative. Two representatives arrived at my home at the scheduled time, and one of the representatives just happened to be the same person that had made the last service call as one of the owners of Company X. Surprise! The representative did have enough integrity to acknowl-edge that he remembered me and the issues with my deck. However, he claimed that he thought it had been taken care of. Once again, they took pictures and said someone would be contacting me. A week passed and no response. I now had the new phone number, so I initiated a phone call. One of the owners happened to answer the phone. He admittedly recognized my name and said he was aware of my issues. He said someone would be out to remedy the problem within a few days. A few days later, a letter arrived that profoundly stated, "We regret that we cannot assist you…and we have placed you on our do not call/mail list for your convenience." Wow!

I contacted an attorney, a dear friend, and he checked the courthouse records and found that there were several court filings against them as well as several bankruptcy filings. We believed legal action would be a waste of time and money. The attorney sent them a letter, and they did respond with a settlement offer that was an insult. I stopped my pursuit for compensation and resolved to take the loss and hire another contractor to redo the deck. This solved my problem.

As the scriptures promises, "It is mine to avenge; I will repay. In due time their foot will slip; their day of disaster is near and their doom rushes upon them" (Deuteronomy 32:35).

I witnessed the demise of the company and the downfall of the owners. I emerged the victor. My faith is a comfort and confirms that "the man of integrity walks securely, but he who takes crooked paths will be found out" (Proverbs 10:9).

# Alarms

If someone asked you to say the first thing that comes to mind when you hear the word *alarm*, what would your response be? Burglar alarm? Fire alarm? Or possibly something totally different. If given some time to think about the question, there would probably be several likely responses.

The dictionary has several definitions of *alarm*: A sudden fear caused by apprehension or realization of danger. A warning of approaching or existing danger. An electrical device or mechanical device that serves to warn of danger by means of a sound or signal.

Some alarms have a very shrill tone and are most often loud—scaring you or causing stress.

Years ago, a very popular sales item for the telephone company was Bell Chimes. For an additional monthly charge, the telephone company would install these Bell Chimes, which replaced the loud "normal" ringing tone of the average telephone. The tone of the bell chime was pleasant and melodious, and if a call came through during the night or early morning, you were less likely to be startled by the tone. It was a sad day for me when the company discontinued this service. I loved my Bell Chimes.

The choice of different alarm settings on clocks is another example of the importance of tones. One can set the clock to buzz, ring, or turn on music. You no longer must awaken to a startling sound from the alarm clock.

Cell phones win the prize. They have more ringtones than I ever thought possible. And having the capacity to assign different tones to specific individuals on the same device is mind-boggling!

Some voices can be very alarming. Especially if someone is screaming or yelling, at you or near you, it can cause apprehension. An abrupt/sharp tone can also trigger an unpleasant feeling. Tones are important. Choosing the right words to say to someone may be a task, but an even greater challenge is the tone used to convey the message.

"A gentle answer turns away wrath, but a harsh word stirs up anger" (Proverbs 15:1).

Do not cause alarm. Keep your tone soft. It will prevent stress and hopefully remind others to maintain calmness!

# America, America: Land of the Free...

$\mathcal{S}$ ince February is designated Black History month, sharing a few facts in a timeline scenario seems appropriate. Some of the names and accomplishments appearing may be familiar; others may be totally obscure. However, even though most are excluded from the American history books—at least when I was in school—they have all made great contributions to our society.

In 1619, twenty Africans arrived in Jamestown, Virginia. They were the first Blacks to be **forcibly settled** in the North American British Colonies.

In 1769, Jean Baptiste Du Sable built a trading post near Lake Michigan. This area would later be known as **Chicago.**

In 1839, an African slave named Joseph Cinque led a successful mutiny aboard the slave ship *Amistad*.

In 1849, **Harriet Tubman** helped three hundred slaves **escape** to freedom.

In 1850, Sojourner Truth dictated her autobiography that was called *The Narrative of Sojourner Truth*.

In 1863, President Abraham Lincoln signed the Emancipation Proclamation:

> That on the 1st day of January, A.D. 1863, all persons held as slaves within any state, or designated part of a state the people whereof shall be then, thenceforward, and forever free; and the executive government of the United States, including the military and naval authority there-

fore, will recognize and maintain the freedom of
such persons...

In 1865, **Juneteenth** marks the anniversary of freed Black slaves
in Texas.

In 1881, Booker T. Washington was chosen to head the new
Tuskegee Institute, a training institute for African American teachers.

1889: Frederick Douglass was named minister-resident and
consul-general to Haiti and the Dominican Republic.

In 1893, Ida B. Wells organized the Ida B. Wells Women's Club.

1896: George Washington Carver became the Tuskegee
Institute's Director of Agricultural Research.

In 1905, W. E. B. DuBois began the Niagara Movement, which
would later be known as the NAACP.

In 1909, Matthew Henson reached the North Pole.

In 1920, Bessie Coleman became the first American woman to
receive an international pilot's license.

In 1939, Marion Anderson performed at the Lincoln memorial.

In 1941, Jacob Lawrence became the first African American art-
ist included in the permanent collection of the Museum of Modern
Art.

In 1942, Dr. Charles Drew became the director of the first
plasma division.

In 1944, Paul Robeson received the Donaldson Award for outstanding lead performance in Othello.

In 1945, *Ebony* magazine was founded by John H. Johnson.

In 1947, Jackie Robinson became the first African American to
play baseball in the major leagues.

In 1950, Ralph Bunche was the first African American to receive
the Nobel Peace Prize.

In 1950, Rosa Parks was arrested for refusing to give up her seat
on the bus.

In 1959, Berry Gordy Jr. opened a recording studio in an apartment, and that was the beginning of Motown Records.

In 1960, Wilma Rudolph won three gold medals in the
Olympics.

In 1963, Martin Luther King Jr. gave his most memorable speech at the March on Washington.

In 1964, Malcolm X formed the Organization of Afro-American Unity.

In 1966, Maulana Ron Karenga created the nonreligious African American holiday of Kwanzaa.

IN 1967, Thurgood Marshall became the first African American US Supreme Court Justice.

In 1968, Shirley Chisolm was elected to the US Congress.

In 1968, Arthur Mitchell started the Dance Theater of Harlem.

In 1969, Clara Hale opened the Hale House (for homeless kids) in Harlem.

In 1971, Jesse Jackson founded a program called PUSH—People United to Save Humanity.

In 1974, Virginia Hamilton received the Newberry Medal for M. C. Higgins, the Great.

In 1975, Arthur Ashe became the first African American to win the men's singles title at Wimbledon.

In 1978, Marva Collins served as Director of the Right to Read Foundation.

In 1989, Colin Powell became chairman of the Joint Chiefs of Staff, the highest military position in the United States.

In 1992, Mae C. Jemison became the first African American woman in space.

In 1995, there was the Million Man March in Washington, DC.

In 1995, Oprah Winfrey was recognized for being the most powerful woman in entertainment.

In 1998, Michael Jordan won his sixth NBA Championship.

With all of the above there have been even greater accomplishments in the 2000s.

The Word of God says, "It is for freedom that Christ has set us free. Stand firm, then, and do not let yourselves be burdened again by a yoke of slavery" (Galatians 5:1).

# Are ANTS Invading Your Space?

The ant is a social insect of the family *Formicidae*. They are determined workers and live in colonies with a complex social organization. There are several species of this pesky insect and they are all extremely annoying. They also have the capacity to be destructive and they are difficult to get rid of once they are established. If you have ever had the opportunity to lay a tablecloth on the grass preparing for a nice picnic lunch, only to find that there is a colony of ants nearby, you understand how they can totally invade your space. What could be worse? The answer is ANTS—automatic negative thoughts!

You have all heard of Debbie Downer. Some of us have a very close relationship with her. If you do, you need to rid yourself of her. On the other hand, we are often guilty of being a self-proclaimed Debbie Downer by entertaining ANTS and letting them invade our and control our lives.

It is the enemy firing flaming darts at you when you let yourself think things like…

Things will never get better.

I will always have this pain.

My kids will never do right.

I will never be happy.

I will never be able to remember all this (as you study for an exam).

I will never be able to break this habit—and as soon as you try, you will do it again.

God does not really care—if He did, He would never have let this happen to me.

God has forgotten me; I am on my own.

So much negativity. Do not do this to yourself. These ANTS interfere with your prayer life, your personal relationships, your health, your devotions, and your general well-being. Fortunately, God has provided and conveniently placed two weapons for us against these ANTS. A **shield** and a **sword**! (2 Corinthians 6:7 and Ephesians 6:16–17).

While the enemy will try to invade your life and your very personal space with these ANTS, if you stand firm in your faith, you will be able to fend off these attacks. Let your faith be your defense and the **WORD** your counterattack. "The weapons we fight with are not the weapons of the world. On the contrary, they have divine power to demolish strongholds. We demolish arguments and every pretension that sets itself up against the knowledge of God, and we take captive every thought to make it obedient to Christ" (2 Corinthians 10:4–5).

Use the weapons at your disposal and claim the promise in 2 Thessalonians 3:3, "The Lord is faithful, and he will strengthen and protect you from the evil one." Kill all the ANTS that are invading your space and be at peace.

# Are You Listening?

With all the advances in technology and mass media, living and listening is hardly a simple task. There is always so much noise—beeps from text messages, musical tones from cell phones, music, and all types of background noises in our environment. Unless you have a secret closet, it is almost impossible to find a quiet place where there are no distractions. All these constant sounds often make it very difficult to hear or to listen. Yet the skill of listening is critical to professional (workplace) success, parenting success, success in school (learning), and spiritual growth.

Years ago, courses and programs on "active listening," were quite popular. In these trainings, we learned that the way one responded in a conversation affirmed that you heard, listened, and understood, what the other person was saying. These training sessions proved to be very difficult and frustrating for some of the participants because they gave immediate responses before they understood what the other person was trying to communicate. Many times, they were guilty of "open mouth, insert foot." In addition, these mock scenarios were very embarrassing for those that were leaders and not accustomed to always "listening." It is difficult to become aware of your own flaws in front of other people. "He who answers before listening—that is his folly and his shame" (Proverbs 18:13). The sessions, however, were very beneficial and helped us to enhance our listening skills.

Listening is designed to increase understanding and improve relationships. Thinking about your spiritual life, are you listening to God? In your daily prayers, are you caught up in a routine ritual where you consistently say the same prayer and then quickly move on to your next task? Do you ever wait and listen for an answer? It is all about having that personal relationship. We know that He knows each of us personally and He may speak to us in various ways. In John 10:27, we learn, "My sheep listen to my voice; I know them, and they follow me."

God may speak to us through a sermon, through scriptures in the Bible, through dreams, or through events or people in our personal lives. Sometimes we may need help to give us direction, so that we can listen and hear, and it is well worth the time and effort. However, it does not stop there. Once we hear and listen, we must learn to obey or adhere to the message or direction we receive. Proverbs 1:5 tells us, "Let the wise listen and add to their learning."

Are you listening? "**Everyone** should be quick to listen, slow to speak, and slow to become angry" (James 1:19).

"Do not merely listen to the word, and so deceive yourselves. Do what it says" (James 1:22).

Think how peaceful the world would be and how much joy we could have, if only more people would learn to listen. Are you listening?

# Are You POOR?

*T*he dictionary has several definitions of poor, and they all refer to some lacking or some deficiency. The Bible references poor many times, and in a variety of contexts. How do you define poor? Did you realize that you may be poor?

In conjunction with the dictionary and the Bible, I propose POOR as an acronym for the following deficiency: *passing over opportunities repeatedly.* In our daily walk, we miss so many opportunities to share, praise, learn, love, and grow. We procrastinate and overlook or obliviously pass by open doors. Why is that? What can we do about our own state of poverty?

In Revelations 3:8, we find these words, "I know your deeds. See, I have placed before you an open door that no one can shut."

When Jesus places doors of opportunities before us, they are not options—they are expectations. We must take every and any opportunity to continually **drink** from His everlasting cup—the Word. We are to **steal** some time to try to improve ourselves, and most definitely steal some time to be with Him. We are to **swear** to give to and help someone less fortunate. We are to **lie** down, praise, and thank God for all His many blessings. We are to **lie** down things that are obstructing our walk. Jesus expects that we drink, steal, swear, and lie at every opportunity.

"Be wise in the way you act toward outsiders; make the most of every opportunity. Let your conversation be always full of grace, seasoned with salt…" (Colossians 4:5–6).

"As we have an opportunity, let us do good to all people…" (Galatians 6:10).

"Be very careful how you live-not as unwise but as wise, making the most of every opportunity..." (Ephesians 5:16).

There is a prayer called The Knot Prayer (author unknown) that may help if you are feeling POOR. It goes like this:

Dear God,

Please untie the knots that are in my mind, my heart, and my life.

Remove the have nots, cannot, and the do nots.

Erase the will nots, may nots, might nots that may find a home in my heart.

Release me from the could nots, would nots, and should nots that obstruct my life.

And most of all, dear God, I ask that you remove from my mind, my heart, and my life all the "am nots" that I have allowed to hold me back. Especially the thought that I am not good enough. Amen.

The scriptures tell us, "There will always be poor people in the land..." (Deuteronomy 15:11, Matthew 26:11, Mark 14:7, and John 12:8). However, the difference is, you have a choice. Decide to drink, steal, swear, and lie. You do not have to be among the POOR.

# Be a Cheerleader

*O*ne of my daughter's favorite activities is scrolling Facebook to visit posted memories from her past. She shared the following enlightenment. Earlier this week, I ran across a video that I posted on Facebook last year around this time. The video used a small child learning to walk to illustrate how important it is to have people in your corner to cheer you on and to encourage you. Even when things may seem like a failure, your cheering section can help you turn things around and set you back on track. The video reminded me of the people that have been in my corner. These people have been placed in my life to not only encourage me but to mold me too. Often, we want to hide our mistakes, but this video pointed out that even when the little guy fell down people cheered. When he heard the cheers of the audience and saw a familiar smile, he stood back up and finished his walk to his smiling mother. This solidified in my mind that while people may not cheer for everything that we do, but when they do, we are forced to reassess how we see our situation.

Victoria Holt penned these words, "Never regret. If it is good, then it is great. If it is bad, then it's an experience." When I saw those words, they resonated with me. I began to think back to several situations and experiences that molded who I am and who I am becoming. Without people who are mindful of you, life can be a lonely journey.

Think back to a time in your life when your cheerleaders pulled you through.

For me, 2015 was one of those times. I needed a cheering section. Thankfully, I had one. Professionally, I was in a dark place. I had a supervisor that was haunting to say the very least. I felt unful-filled. Overly scrutinized. I was unhappy. My growth was stunted.

Physically, I needed to make changes. My weight hit an all-time high, and I was experiencing stress related health issues. My mental state was negatively affecting me physically and spiritually.

Spiritually, I had fallen. Sunday was reserved for mourning the upcoming Monday and devoted to eating fatty foods and binging on TV shows or movies. I would sit in my recliner and think through how I was going to make through the next day...

But God. God led me to a devotional journal. One thing that I have always enjoyed is writing, and this devotional gave me an outlet toward healing. This devotional was a gift from my mother. She was and continues to be my cheerleader. There are others, even when I did not know...they were cheering and continues to cheer.

Today, that dark time feels like ages ago. my progression has been monumental. Just know that your encouragement and support may help someone look up and see a different path for their life.

"Therefore, encourage and build each other up" (1 Thessalonians 5:11).

Be a cheerleader!

# Be Grateful

*W*e are all familiar with the cliché, "'Tis the season to be jolly!" Ponder that thought, and look over your life, as it is today, as it was in the past, and possibly, what the future may hold. Without a doubt, there have been many changes. Moreover, if you continue living, there will be more changes—some good and maybe some, not so good. However, life goes on. Are you grateful for life?

Truly the Christmas season seems to open the hearts of many and subsequently they are more willing, at this time the year, to help those less fortunate, to share with family and friends, to pleasantly greet others, and to show their love and or generosity. Did you ever wonder why that happens just once a year? Is all this for show or are we truly grateful that we can share?

At this time of the year, all the stores are very accommodating. Not only do they offer twenty-four-hour service, but also there are all kinds of coupons, lay-away plans, discounts, and various incentives to get you to buy more. In addition, unfortunately—I think—most consumers fall for the merchandising gimmicks. There is a tendency to overspend, overeat, over drink all under the guise of "'Tis the season to be jolly!"

A few months ago, Pastor did an outstanding series on "Be Thankful." Those sermons and teachings led to making you truly look at yourself and the life you are living. When you look up thankful in the dictionary, it is almost synonymous with grateful. However, the dictionary defines grateful as being "appreciative of benefits received." How grateful are you?

When you get up each morning, are you thankful and grateful? You may have had a restless night, bad dreams, bathroom calls, etc., but you made it through the night. Are you grateful that you were able to get out of bed and start another day?

I challenge you to start looking at all that you do have, instead of what you may not have, and just be grateful! If you have a headache, be grateful that your back is not hurting. If your legs hurt, give them a rest while you use the hands that are still working well! Be grateful for what you have! Be grateful for everything you got! Think on those things you have, and it will take your mind off what you might want.

God said He would never leave you nor forsake you, so you can count on that. Be grateful for that!

'Tis the season to be jolly. Continue to give, share, and love. Be thankful that you can. Pray to have eyes that see the best in people, a heart that forgives the worst, a mind that forgets the bad and a soul that never loses faith in God.

May the God of hope fill you with all joy and peace in believing, so that by the power of the Holy Spirit, you may abound in hope and be grateful! (2 Corinthians 9:15).

Wishing you a wonderful holiday season and a joyous New Year. Merry Christmas.

# A Mosquito or a Bee?

*T*oday is a brand-new day. How will you start your day? We have choices to make, an agenda to attack, and things to do. Do you start the day with a "to-do" list or do you pray for God's will to order your steps?

Will this be a day to get some rest and relaxation, read, binge watch TV or play Word with Friends? Maybe it is a day to go shopping, or a day for house cleaning. There may be some cooking, meetings, telephone calls to make, etc. Will you choose to study His Word? Will you choose to take time to pray? Will you invest in a physical workout or spiritual strengthening? It is possible to do just about any combination of these activities, but where you spend your time is indicative of where your heart lies.

Our "to-do" list may include a variety of tasks. Bottom line—we are busy all day! Often, I must remind myself to work smarter not harder, but the tasks mount up. The book of Matthew reminds us, "Come to me, all who labor and are heavy laden, and I will give you rest."

For clarification turn in your Bible to Luke 10:38–42. Jesus praises Mary for looking to God to order her steps. Mary chooses to sit as Jesus's feet rather than to busy herself with daily tasks. Martha finds herself frustrated with Mary for not helping her prepare or complete their daily chores. Mary is busy, but not busy like Martha would like her to be. Mary understood the importance of taking time to listen. Sometimes listening and being still is what we need to do. The dictionary defines busy as "being actively engaged in some form of work, occupied." Mary was occupied with the splendor of God.

The question remains, are you more like Mary or Martha…a bee, busy making honey, or a mosquito, busy stinging people and creating hurt? Actions speak louder than words, and our behavior is a testimony of who we are and whose we are.

There are probably days that the "to-do" list out numbers the hours in a day—leaving us stressed and disappointed. However, if we learn to pray and trust our "to-do" list to God, the circumstances of the day and our life will be a beautiful tapestry instead of a tangled mess of threads. How good is that?

Look around you. If God can manage the stars in the sky, the precise orbiting of the planets, the intricacies of the cycles of life, I suspect He can manage and guide us through the busyness of our day.

Think about this: Did Jesus come to earth to help us get more done and cross things off a "to-do" list? I do not think so! His life, death, and resurrection made it possible for us to have a personal relationship with God—walking and talking with Him. Jesus wants our love for Him before He wants our work for Him.

"Some among you are idle. They are not busy; they are busybodies" (2 Thessalonians 3:11).

Do not let busyness overtake your worship and love for Jesus!

Let us make **bee** busy our focus—making honey!

# Been Too Long

*A*s a child, you possibly spent hours or days making that special birthday or Christmas gift for a parent or a sibling. Completing that thoughtful gift of macaroni art, finger-painting, string art, or weaving a potholder took time, patience, and love. How meaningful was this gift as compared to the "gift card" purchase of today? How much time, effort, and thought went into that purchase?

When was the last time you celebrated someone (living) joyously, or paid honor to someone, freely showing love? It seems to me; this most often happens when the celebrant is not able to hear or enjoy the accolades or feel the love! Why not show that love when you both can benefit from the expressions and experience?

When was the last time you had a physical exam? That pain that surfaces periodically is warning you about something. Get it checked before it is too late.

Blurred vision? Eye examines need to be included in your schedule of preventive health measures. Been too long?

Are your teeth important to you? When was the last time you saw a dentist? Has it been too long ago?

Do you have the television blasting loud enough for the neighbors to censor your media choices? It must be time for an ear exam or at least a cleaning and wax removal.

Do you spend family evenings sitting in front of the television and communicating with others by sending text messages? How long has it been since you played a board game and indulged in vocal conversations—no texting? This kind of activity helps with communications and in building relationships. The time spent sharing, talking, and competing provides a comfortable atmosphere of closeness that allows for connecting and sharing. It also helps to develop social skills. We spend too much time with social media. Get back to family time. Been too long...

When was the last time you gave yourself kudos? Can you remember a time when you said, "Self, good job"? When you do a good job, and deserve a pat on the back, give it to yourself! Why not? "The cheerful heart has a continual feast" (Proverbs 15:15).

How long has it been since you contacted an ailing relative who may need just an encouraging word? If you cannot visit, a phone call will do wonders. Do not continue to put it off.

Most of us are busy and have many interests and activities, but there are many things that affect others, loved ones, friends, us—that need our attention.

A challenge would be—make of list of those things that you have been ignoring or have put on the backburner for a later time. Review that list, pray over it, and decide what has been there too long. Getting rid of "been too long" things might be just what is needed to help you get on with your life! Live and enjoy each day as though it was your last. Be happy—do not worry!

# Blissipline

*A*nyone that knows me well, knows that I love Scrabble. It is, by far, one of the things that brings me joy at any time of the day or night. Searching for new words, which an opponent, may not know, is fun and makes me happy! This brings me to "blissipline."

During my daily devotions, I came across *blissipline*, a new word to me. This word was defined as choosing to do things that make you happy, and that will guarantee you success. It is basically the opposite of discipline. The basis of the writing centered on New Year's resolutions. According to many surveys, New Year's resolutions do not offer a lot of success. By the end of January, many resolutions have fallen by the wayside, and by the end of July, most are gone. Although the resolutions are most likely worthy goals, they are often burdensome, and things that others may have coerced you into making. These self-imposed obligations are most often disciplinary and gives us an attitude of "something I have to do" as opposed to something that brings you joy.

Achieving those set goals, brings a certain amount of satisfaction, but does it give you joy?

Making choices from the heart as opposed to from the head changes the total outlook and gives an entirely different perspective. You will be doings things for joy rather than out of obligation. What a difference!

This article stressed paying more attention to New Year's evolutions. Thus, allowing you to be on a trajectory of awakening, healing, and self-expression. This is achieved because you are being true to yourself and "letting life live through you rather than marching into the black hole of endless obligation."

When you are living and doing your choices, and not just trying to please others, success is the only option!

Following the principle of blissipline may be just what is needed to help us resolve to evolve. Make the choice at the beginning of each new year to take steps to live better physically, emotionally, and spiritually. Live blissfully! "Oh, restore me to health and make me live" (Isaiah 38:16).

# Bon Appétit

One morning while scanning the newspaper, an article entitled "**Teala**" caught my attention. The article is about a recipe that sounds delightful and one I would like to try. I was not familiar with the word *Teala*, but I was eager to add it to my memory bank for playing Words with Friends or Scrabble. However, Teala does not appear in either the *American Heritage Dictionary* or the *Official Scrabble Dictionary*. Therefore, I will not be able to use it in a Scrabble game, but with Words with Friends, who knows. Words with Friends accepts many words with the disclaimer—no valid definition, but acceptable with Words with Friends! Not fair!

The other reason this article attracted me was that the word reminded me of a very pleasant previous experience. On a visit to Las Vegas, we had the opportunity to enjoy a meal in a little restaurant named Taibbi (pronounced *tee-yee-bee*). While there, through posted signs and conversations with the staff, we learned the meaning of the word. When used as a verb, Taibbi means to inspire and be inspired, to connect to the community through inspirational creations. As a noun, it means the embodiment of inspiration. Lastly, it is an acronym for "to inspire and be inspired." And it is truly that!

The atmosphere at Taibbi was pleasant, comfortable, and energizing. The staff was friendly, accommodating, and efficient. In addition, the food was excellent. The specialty of this quaint little restaurant was waffles—all kinds of waffles. The staff respectfully refer to the waffles as pancakes with abs—Taibbi—the embodiment of inspiration. In addition to the wide variety of waffles, they have a great choice of exotic drinks—flavored teas, coffee, juices, and milk drinks.

This little restaurant was an inspirational experience. We were a group of five, and this was the only eating experience we had during our week stay, where no one had a complaint or any negativity. It was a happy, pleasant, and satisfying experience, as we shared and learned. So if given the opportunity to visit Las Vegas, look up and visit this quaint little restaurant. I believe you will be pleased and blessed by the environment and the food. I am reminded of Hebrews 5:14, "Solid food is for the mature, who by constant use have trained themselves to distinguish from good from evil." Bon appetit!

# Caring for Your Heart

*I*t seems that we cannot turn on the TV, radio, or open the mail without seeing some type of promotion about physical fitness. There seems to be as many fitness centers as there are gas stations. These facilities are patronized not only by those intent on building better bodies, but often by those who are looking for a warm friendly place to socialize—and not break a sweat! Therefore, depending on your interest, you might want to do some checking of the facility before you join. It is probably a good idea to see if the facility has a visitor's pass option before making a commitment to join. At any rate, there are choices.

So often, the visits to the fitness centers are primarily for cardio workouts. Many folks are now giving serious thought to the state of their hearts. Sometimes this is a planned effort for preventive measures; however, all too often, the fitness center visits come after a heart attack or some other major warning sign. It does, however, seem that we are becoming more aware of preventive measures. And that is a good thing!

Mentioning the heart, one's mind might quickly go to fitness, cardio-workouts, heart disease, warning signs, or risk factors for heart disease.

Some may immediately think about the "heart" being the most important or essential part of something or someone. Whether we are discussing the body, the financial system, or problems, getting to and knowing the significant part is crucial; and the "heart" is that vital center.

The human heart is a fantastic, muscular organ that pumps blood received from the veins into arteries, thereby supplying our entire circulatory system. Our heart also has the capacity for sympathy, compassion, and love. Therein lies our strength!

While there is much concern with better bodies and muscle tone, we must also keep our spiritual hearts strengthened. We do this by reading and studying the scriptures and receiving the message of God's goodness and grace. Our priority should be, must be, keeping our spiritual heart strong and fit. Martin Luther King once said, "The belief that God will do everything for man is as untenable as the belief that man can do everything for himself. It, too, is based on a lack of faith. We must learn that to expect God to do everything while we do nothing is not faith but superstition." So…going to the gym or fitness center and not breaking a sweat, is not going to tone our muscles or strengthen our cardio. As caretakers of our bodies, we must use some wisdom.

1 Timothy 4:8 tells us, "Physical training is of some value, but godliness has value for all things, holding promise for both the present life and the life to come."

Care for your heart by strengthening it with grace!

# Celebrating and Valuing the Life and Legacy of Dr. Martin Luther King Jr.

*I*n January, there is a day designated to observe Dr. King's birthday. Many cities, churches, and universities plan activities to recall the courage and challenges of this great civil rights leader who suffered and died for his beliefs. The "I Have a Dream" speech is well known and seems to be the focal point for most of those celebrating Dr. King's Life. But there is so much more.

When Dr. King confronted those who dealt out injustice, he and his followers were stopped, jailed, ridiculed, threatened, and sometimes beaten. They were called rabble-rousers, communists, disturbers of the peace and worse. While he had many supporters, the majority stood by and did not a thing!

I believe we should recall and remember that Dr. King chose not to remain silent in the face of injustice. Can we say the same about ourselves? When you witness anyone treated without respect, without fair play, without kindness or without Christian love, do you remain mute? How much more inner peace we would have if we would follow the suggestion of Dr. King: "With our faith, we will transform the jangling discords of our nation into a beautiful symphony of brotherhood." Let us take some time to reflect upon this and some of Dr. King's wise sayings and suggestions:

> We will have to repent in this generation not merely for the hateful words and actions of the bad people but for the appalling silence of the good people.

I have decided to stick with love. Hate is too great a burden to bear.

We must accept finite disappointment, but we must never lose infinite hope.

The ultimate measure of a man is not where he stands in moments of comfort and convenience, but where he stands at times of challenge and controversy.

I refuse to accept the view that mankind is so tragically bound to the starless midnight of racism and war that the bright daybreak of peace and brotherhood can never become a reality. I believe that unarmed truth and unconditional love will have the final word.

We must learn to live together as brothers or perish as fools.

We must come to see that human progress never rolls in on wheels of inevitability. It comes through the tireless efforts and persistent work of people willing to be coworkers with God...

Take the first step in faith. You do not have to see the whole staircase. Just take the first step.

There is so much frustration in the world because we have relied on gods rather than God. We have genuflected (bent our knees) before the god of science only to find that it has given us the atomic bomb... We have worshipped the god of pleasure only to discover that thrills play out and sensations are short-lived. We have bowed before the god of money only to learn that there are such things as love and friendship that money cannot buy and that, in a world of possible depressions, stock market crashes and bad business investments, money is a rather uncertain deity. These transitory gods are not able to save or bring hap-

piness to the human heart. Only God is able. It is
faith we must rediscover.

True, Dr. King's life was short and ended abruptly. However,
that little dash, between his birth date and date of death, on his
tombstone, carries more teachings, hopes, lessons of faith and love
than any of us will ever achieve. Let us do more than celebrate Dr.
King's life, let us value his legacy.

"Love must be sincere. Hate what is evil; cling to what is good.
Be devoted to one another in brotherly love. Honor one another
above yourselves" (Romans 12:9–10).

# Celebrating Ethnicity

*P*ablo Picasso once said, "I begin with an idea and then it becomes something."

Earl Nightengale stated, "Everything begins with an idea."

In addition, a song says, "It only takes a spark to get a fire going…"

All these references relate to a discussion that occurred in the spring of 1990 when the Kelly Miller Alumni Association met to do some brainstorming about fundraising. That discussion led to the beginning and commemoration of "The Emancipation Proclamation Celebration." The "Emancipation Celebration" was the dream child of Deacon Allen Lee (deceased). Deacon Lee was born and raised in Clarksburg and attended Kelly Miller School. After graduation from Kelly Miller, he entered the military and then found successful employment in the garment industry in New York. Upon retirement, Deacon Lee returned to Clarksburg and it was through his efforts that the "Emancipation Celebration" was born. This celebration took place on or near September 22, 1990, on Water Street (currently, E. B. Saunders Way), right here in Clarksburg. After a few successful years, noted by increased attendance, interest, and support the celebration evolved into what is now known as the West Virginia Black Heritage Festival (WVBHF).

Many years later, the idea is still growing. Moreover, dreams have become a reality. The festival serves as a conduit that brings the entire community together to fellowship and work together for the common good, in a family-type atmosphere. Initially there were approximately ten to twelve local vendors, featuring art, crafts, ethnic foods, and local musicians. The festival now entertains approximately fifty vendors from surrounding states, diverse ethnicity in foods, nationally known artists and authors, plus nationally known music recording artists.

Financial backing from loyal supporters, contributions from local organizations and businesses and faithful volunteers make the festival a reality. Although the supporters have grown over the years, from its meager beginnings, the Festival has been able to rely on support from the following:

- John Ebert and the McDonald Corp along with Fairmont State University for co-sponsoring the youth activities on Friday evening
- Outback Steak House as sponsors of the pre-festival fundraising luncheon
- City of Clarksburg
- Harrison County Commission
- Harrison County Board of Education
- Harry Green Chevrolet Nissan
- The State of West Virginia
- Davis Funeral Home
- Dominion Hope
- Pierpont Community College
- Clarksburg Visitors Bureau

In honor of the twenty-fifth anniversary, the WVBHF moved to Main Street, Downtown Clarksburg. Mark your calendars for the second weekend in September for a Block Party for Youth on Friday evening. The opening ceremony is scheduled for twelve noon, Saturday, at the Courthouse Plaza. Ronald McDonald may even make an appearance to visit with the youth on Saturday afternoon. Live entertainment normally begins at 2:00 PM on Saturday, with local groups, followed by nationally renowned groups the remainder of the evening.

On Sunday, a Community Church Service is scheduled for 11:00 AM at the Courthouse Plaza, followed by a Gospel Explosion!

For information that is more detailed and to view current happenings, visit the website: www.wvbhf.com.

Sincere thanks to all our supporters, volunteers, and contributors! The festival would not be possible without your loyalty and concern to make this community a better place to live.

Help keep the celebration going for years to come. "For generations to come you shall celebrate it as a festival to the Lord..." (Exodus 12:14).

# Chain Reactions

*The American Heritage Dictionary* defines a "chain reaction" as a series of events each of which induces or influences its successor. It also gives the following definition: A series of reactions in which one product of a reacting set is a reactant in the following set. To get a good mental visual of a chain reaction, picture the *domino effect*, where several rows of dominoes stand on end, and when one is pushed, they all fall in succession—chain reaction.

It seems many things around us today might be classified as "chain reactions." The drug epidemic and the continuous blatant misuse of the killer fentanyl for example. One person succumbs and their friends or associates follow even though they know the possible outcome. Another example is the following of news events on Facebook, such as the birth of the baby giraffe last week. Millions signed onto Facebook to witness the birth and to see the newborn. Amazing!

A few years ago, Rachel's Challenge was a popular "chain reaction." Rachel Scott, the first student murdered in the Columbine High School Tragedy in 1999, had written a profound challenging essay one month before her death. The essence of Rachel's essay was about her goal was to reach out to three groups of students that are often neglected: those that were handicapped, those that were new at school, those who were picked on and put down by others. The essay was a challenge to her readers to "start a chain reaction of kindness and compassion." After her death, this challenge developed into a school assembly and training program. Schools across America as well as Canada, Australia, Bermuda, and other countries participated in this challenge. There are many heart-warming stories and testimonies of the positive impact of this chain-reaction.

Have you ever had a loose thread hanging from a hemline, and without thinking, you pull that thread? That thread happens to be looped with all the other threads holding that seam in place, and suddenly, you have an open seam or hemline! Chain reaction!

A prayer chain is a powerful example of a chain reaction. When one person gets the call for prayer, the information is passed on and on and on. Prayers go up and miracles happen. Healings occur. Family restorations take place. Addictions are pushed aside. Freedom prevails. It is like the domino effect. With that first nudge, as the dominoes fall, and the prayers go up, all the issues fall aside!

Why do we wait for a crisis or illness to start a prayer chain? Think about randomly picking someone and starting the prayer chain for a blessed and fruitful day. That someone might be a loved one, a friend, or your pastor. You could get a prayer movement started! Remember, it only takes a spark to get a fire going!

A sincere prayer brings wonderful results. "Pray for each other… The prayer of a righteous man is powerful and effective" (James 5:16).

# Chains That Bind

*W*hen you hear the word *chain*, you possibly get a visual of metal links that are locked together to make a strong flexible line. Right off the bat, you may think of a 14 karat gold necklace or bracelet. That is a pleasant thought.

However, you may also picture men in striped suits, legs linked together—prisoners on a chain gang. Another visual might be from the movies, where you see immigrants chained to ships or in trucks being hauled across the borders. Whatever visual you may see; it is obvious that these chains are restraints than confine and restrict freedom.

Chains are an anchor. Think about the restrictive nature of the chains that are visible. Then think about all the invisible chains that invade our lives and bodies, binding us in pain. Chain-smoking is most often visible, although some try to hide the habit. I am thinking of the somewhat invisible chains that shackle our hearts, minds, and bodies to the point that puts distance between you and others. Things like living and staying in an abusive relationship. Being isolated from family and friends. Being in a situation where one person dominates the other in so many aspects of their lives. Then there is the aspect of stalking—which is another type of chain. It produces fear and often handicaps or prevents you from leading a normal life.

Internal turmoil is very common today. Internal turmoil causes such pain that it often led to such things as homelessness, addictions, desperateness, and abuse of others. Harboring unforgiveness is another very strong invisible chain.

What can we do about these chains? First, we must stop and take care of the pain. Face the pain, invisible chain, and admit its reality. This is not an easy task, but once we do it, we can begin to work through it. Next, we must trace the source of the pain—invisible chain—in our lives. Many times, this may require an outside objective observer to help identify or pinpoint things we do not see or won't see in our lives. Finally, we need to "grace" the pain. Put it in its proper place. Give it to God. 2 Corinthians 12:9, God told Paul, "My grace is sufficient for thee; for my strength is made perfect in weakness." In effect, He says, "My grace will be with you in your fiery furnace, my grace will help you part the waters of your Jordan Rivers. My grace will shut the mouths of the lions in your lion's den. My grace will fight your battles and bring down the walls of your Jerichoans."

Whatever chains, visible or invisible, are obstructing your freedom and holding you in bondage, know that God is able to give you the strength to make it through, but you have to take time to deal with the pain. Break the chains. Read Mark 5:1–20 for some great examples.

# Changing Seasons

*N*ormally when we enter the fourth calendar month of the year, April, there is a positive reminder of the changing seasons—winter to spring. This is the time to plant. This is a time for "new beginnings." A time for better weather—so we hope. However, with every change, there is usually both a positive and a supposed negative. The third chapter of Ecclesiastes clearly explains, there is a season for every activity—more or less—a circle for life.

On the positive side, we joyously celebrate a new birth, and on the opposite side, we mourn a death. So in essence, there is a time to laugh and a time to weep.

In life, individually, we change physically, as we go through the different seasons of maturity. We may encounter many changes in any given season, and sometimes even the different seasons overlap. In addition, at each season of life, we most often have a different perspective on the important things in our lives. In infancy, we are totally dependent on others for survival.

As we move forward to the toddler and childhood stages and grow more independent, the dependency needs may be more inclined toward safety. Moving forward to the stages of youth, teenage, young adult, and mature adult, the circle widens but continues to move going back toward the beginning. The perspectives and dependency change also. Experiencing something at the age of eighteen, and the same thing at the age of forty is overwhelming different.

The changes that occur with the weather and the yearly seasonal changes are natural. We can do little about the coming of rain, snow, icy roads, earthquakes, tsunamis, etc. While we have the capacity to react to these occurrences, the control of how much it rains, or snows is out of our hands. Life is different, we cannot just lie, and wait, we must act. Reading gives us knowledge. Living and life give us wisdom and understanding.

It is living that helps us to understand such sayings as "Life is fragile, handle it with prayer"; "Love deeply, laugh heartily, and pray daily"; and "Prayer changes things and people."

What is your season? Where are you in this circle of life? What are you doing with your life? As you go through your seasons and the changes that go with each season, rest assured that the one constant is, "Jesus Christ, the same yesterday and today and forever" (Hebrews 13:8).

# Cherish the Moments

It is estimated that the average person takes about twenty-one thousand breaths a day without even thinking about it. It is one thing not to notice each breath, but it is entirely another thing not to take them! We all know the alternative to not breathing! Do not take me there yet!

Try this. Breathe deep into your abdomen. Exhale slowly. Do this about ten times. How does concentrating on each breath feel? Do you feel more relaxed? Do you feel refreshed? Are you exhausted? Imagine what life would be like if we had to concentrate on and think twenty-one thousand times each day to breathe. Please learn to be grateful for and cherish each breath!

In Job 33:4, it confirms, "The spirit of God hath made me, and the breath of the Almighty hath given me life." Live on! Cherish each breathe!

Picture a chain-smoker and visualize how they are not only polluting the air that you and I breathe but think about the damage they are doing to their own bodies. Perhaps if each package of cigarettes were to show a picture of healthy lungs on one side and a picture of smoke-damaged lungs on the other side, people would become more conscious and concerned about the health risks associated with smoking. Just maybe! If you have ever been in a room full of smokers, seated in, or passed through a smoking area, it won't take much for you to imagine the stifling effect of the secondhand smoke. Cherish your breath—even when others do not cherish theirs! Move to a cleaner environment!

Seeing someone confined to the use of oxygen is a situation that reminds one to be grateful and cherish each breath.

You may have heard someone say, "That took my breath away." What exactly do they mean? Might it be better to say, "That took me by surprise?" I do not know, maybe. Our breathing is not just important, it is critical! Do not let anyone or anything, astound you—take your breath away!

Surely, you can think of instances when you became short of breath—maybe walking too fast, running to catch a bus, or even climbing a hill. When your breathing returned to normal, did you appreciate the fact that you could breathe? Some things will make you think about and appreciate "normal" breathing.

When watching TV and you see someone being smothered to death, do you have empathy for that person? Can you feel their life drifting away? What about when someone is consumed by fire. The hot flames block the oxygen and heat fills the lungs! Wow! Can you imagine that feeling?

A few years ago, there was a popular secular song with lyrics, "Every breath you take, every move you make, I'll be watching you…" He is watching over us, and every breath we take and every move we make is in the Almighty's hand.

Read John 20:22. Cherish each breath, knowing the next one is not promised, and remember, "Always give yourselves fully to the work of the Lord, because you know that your labor in the Lord is not in vain" (1 Corinthians 15:58).

# Choices: Is It Worth It?

*E*ach day we are faced with making choices. Some of the choices are so routine that they are now officially habits. Some choices can and often do have a great and lasting impact on our lives. How many times have you acted on an impulse and later regretted the choice you made? If only I could do that over again, is a thought that we can all identify with. The truth is, not often do we get to do it over again. When consciously faced with a choice, how much better off we would be, if we would only take the time and ask ourselves, "Is it worth it?"

Your day does not start until you have that cup of coffee. You probably do not even consider the choice of the other hot beverages that might be available and may possibly even be better for you. How do you like your coffee? Will you use sugar or a sweetener? Do you choose cream or leave it black? Choices, choices, choices. What impact, if any, will your choice have on your daily dietary intake?

Do you most often wear a smile or a frown? The expression you share can have either a positive or a negative reaction. Just remember it takes more muscles to frown, and frowning causes wrinkles while smiles cause twinkles in your eyes. Is a frown worth getting wrinkles?

Those few extra pounds that you hate to see when you look in the mirror, or when you are trying on new clothes, did not just appear without you making a choice...exercise or "couch potato"? Is having control over the remote worth it? Just think how much better you would feel and look if you took a daily walk instead of just "running" to get the remote. Poor food choices—biscuits and gravy versus wheat toast. Is it worth it?

These may seem like small things, but they can greatly influence our quality of life.

Now picture this. There is a large silver platter of choices placed before you. As you look more closely, the items are all labeled. The selections are emphysema, cancer, heart disease, obesity, diabetes, STD, and HIV. You can have your choice. Would you be anxious to select? I think not. When given this choice, I believe we would all think first and hopefully realize that our choices do determine our destiny. If we want to be healthy and happy, know that "if it's to be—it's up to me."

In Joshua 24:14–15 we find these words: "Fear the Lord and serve Him with all faithfulness. Throw away the gods your forefathers worshiped...and serve the Lord... Choose for yourselves this day whom you will serve..." Make your choices worth choosing!

# Choose Joy

What is joy? The *Biblical Encyclopedia* defines *joy* as "the criterion of health whereby all the powers and affections are enriched and harmonized—the satisfaction of the soul at attaining its desire." In other words, joy is that fountain of internal peace that can only come through a relationship with Jesus Christ.

Too often, we confuse joy and happiness. Happiness being that feeling induced by external objects, events and/or people. These feelings are temporary and last for varying degrees of time. However, they do not satisfy your soul, and often leave you searching for something more. Searching for *happiness*—defined in *Webster* as enjoying, marked by pleasure or joy, cheerful, well adapted, a spontaneous or obsessive inclination—leads many down roads they really do not want to travel. Searching for tangible/material things to provide happiness is like looking for love in all the wrong places. Some may try drugs. Some turn to alcohol. Some turn to pornography or illicit sex. The market for sin is varied and wide. The choices can be enticing—but not satisfying, and most often very harmful.

The end of summer seems to be a trying time. Parents and guardians are dealing with several back-to-school issues—finances, school tuition, school shopping, after school care, etc. In addition, the day light hours are getting shorter. These stressors and season changes cause many to experience "seasonal affective disorder." Seeking happy may lead to many unresolved issues and unhappiness. Would you agree that what many people call happy is counterfeit joy?

The song "Jesus is the Center of my Joy" adequately describes joy versus happy.

## Center of My Joy
### Richard Smallwood

Jesus, you're the center of my joy
All that's good and perfect comes from you
You're the heart of my contentment, hope for all I do
Jesus, you're the center of my joy
When I've lost my direction, you're the compass for my way
You're the fire and light when nights are long and cold
In sadness, you are the laughter, that shatters all my fears
When I'm all alone, your hand is there to hold, ohh
Jesus, you're the center of my joy
All that's good and perfect comes from you
You're the heart of my contentment, hope for all I do
Jesus, you're the center of my joy
You are why I find pleasure in the simple things in life
You're the music in the meadows and the streams
The voices of the children, my family, and my home
You're the center of my joy…

Choose joy and cast all your cares and burdens on the One who can and will take care of them for you. "You have filled my heart with greater joy than when their grain and new wine abound. I will lie down and sleep in peace, for you alone, O LORD, make me dwell in safety" (Psalms 4:7–8).

# Choose Your Fitness

*A*s fads come and go, one of today's popular fads is fitness. In addition, to just looking trim and slim, there is an emphasis on healthy choices.

There are constant mass media ads displaying different weight loss programs, weight loss drugs, fitness programs, body makeover offers, healthy food choice options, and even body-sculpting possibilities. It seems to be all about self-images and choices. Billboards advertise some of the same choices as television and radio. There is a joint effort to make you more conscious of your body image. If you have the "right" body, there are all kinds of opportunities available to you—good health, love, sex, friendship, and happiness!

Gyms and spas offer free trial memberships with trainers to assist you with your mission. This enticement often leads to long-term memberships.

There are also many "home" exercise programs, CDs, television programs, and a wide variety of equipment choices available for purchase. This equipment, supposedly, will help you get into the fitness routine. In lieu of purchasing weights, for example, using sixteen-ounce cans of food make a great substitute for one-pound weights. Using your creative skills could save a few dollars, and still get the job done.

Cell phones and computers have "apps" available to help track and monitor such things as calorie intake, exercise, and steps taken. These aps record and track almost anything—once the proper formulas are in place. If you can master down-loading the aps and getting the formulas in place, all you need do is input the data, and anything or everything you want to know about your life style is available at your fingertips, with the touch of the right button.

One could assume that any weight issue could be tackled and overcome with the right AP. I think we all know what assume can mean!

Exercise is a big part of the fitness process. Depending on one's medical condition, various physical exercises are an option. Many take on running, jogging, or my favorite, walking. Running and/or jogging shakes and juggles body parts that in my opinion do not need the activity. Walking is gentler and it is relaxing.

There are television programs offering various exercise regimes specifically for those with medical issues. There are quick workout options where one can do ten-minute activities three to four times a day. Another suggested option is simply flexing muscles, like rotating ankles or bending feet, to keep circulation flowing—especially if you are in a sitting or reclining position for an extended period. Flexing the muscles is quite helpful as preventive therapy for clotting issues.

It seems that the three most important things to consider for a fit, healthy life are food choices, exercise, and rest. Check labels and try to make wise food choices. Aim for eight hours of sleep each night and plan for regular physical activity.

Please make sure that your exercise is truly physical and not the following:

- Running your mouth
- Pushing your luck
- Jumping to conclusions

Make healthy choices. Be blessed. "Choose life, so that you and your children may live" (Deuteronomy 30:19).

# Choose to Be Free

We live in a fast-paced world where change is constant, and we are continually letting "things" and/or people rule and ruin our daily lives. For example, modern technology and instant communication devices have created yet another "addiction." This generation has become "slaves" to iPhones, texting, web cameras, Facebook, etc. A misplaced, lost, or malfunctioning cell phone will cause many to have an anxiety attack, if not a complete "meltdown." But if we believe the scripture, "only what you do for Christ will last," why are we conjoined to our cell phone like Siamese twins?

Over the past several months, I have shared thoughts on such topics as "When given lemons, make lemonade," "Decisions determine our destiny, and "One hundred days of happy," and now I am urging you to "Choose to be free." This means make a deliberate decision to not let anybody or anything steal your joy! This also means that each day is a new beginning! Just like you shower and put on clean clothes each morning, refresh your attitude also. This may require an attitude adjustment, but rely on Romans 12:2, "Renew your mind and you shall be transformed…" Choose to be free. Opt for an attitude of gratitude for another day and pray for God's will to be done in your life this day.

Start the day in faith with a "Good morning Lord," instead of "Oh, Lord, it's morning." A positive mindset will set the stage for a more pleasant day and a more pleasant you! As the song says, "Rise, shine, and give God the glory…" You are now off to a good start!

Do not make excuses and start complaining. Look for good. Yes, it is raining, and you had plans to work in the yard. So instead of "Hello, sunshine, it is good to see you," our morning greeting is

"Good morning, rain, we needed you." This will be a good day to clean a closet. Keep your mind going in a positive direction and you will find yourself healthier, happy, and with more energy. We know the world is in a constant state of change, so we need to be flexible enough to change also. If you have a few aches and pains, and who does not, get busy and you will soon forget about the aches. When your mind is going in the right direction, your life will follow suit! Choose to be free! It all begins with a "new attitude." "Do not conform any longer to the pattern of this world but be transformed by the renewing of your mind. Then you will be able to test and approve what God's will is—His good, pleasing and perfect will" (Romans 12:2).

# Christmas Reflections

The Christmas season is one of my favorite times of the year. Even though there have been some sad times and tragedies within the family during this season, remembering the reason for the season outweighs all the bad. "For in Him we live and move and have our being" (Acts 17:28).

Reflecting on my childhood, there are memories of family fun times in the kitchen. There would be bags of mixed nuts in the shell and walnuts in the shell. We would sit around the kitchen table cracking and chopping nuts for the baking. One of my other memories is picking walnuts from the tree, letting them dry and trying to crack them with a hammer. Talking about using a little elbow grease! Some of the nuts were so hard Daddy had to help. There were special round containers with a holder for a nutcracker and that is where the mixed nuts were displayed. Several days were spent baking cookies, pound cakes, pies, and fruitcakes. The fruitcakes required extra attention, because periodically rum was poured over it. I do not know if the rum was a preservative, for flavor, or both. It was a task to be done. Once the baking was done, we filled Christmas tins with a variety of cookies and homemade candy to share with neighbors and friends. That was neat!

Our Christmas savings checks gave us the opportunity to go shopping for gifts. Our favorite place was G. C. Murphy's 5 & 10 cents store. We bought handkerchiefs, games, body lotions, scarves, wrapping paper, etc.—big spenders! All this preparation was done as we anxiously awaited the arrival of our older siblings coming home for the holidays. One brother was in the navy, one was in the air force, and my two sisters were working in Washington, DC. Everyone would be home for Christmas. Also included in our family gathering were an aunt and uncle who rode the train in from Pittsburgh. It was always an exciting time. Remembering and reflecting on these times, the top priority was the inside of the house. China had to be washed, silver polished, special tablecloths ironed, and a live tree and other decorations specifically placed. Compare that to getting our hearts and minds ready for a relationship with our Savior. What a worthwhile and rewarding objective. Those times are still a very clear visual. Studying lines for the Christmas play or memorizing a speech for the Christmas program was a part of the season.

Moving on to when I became a parent, most of the traditions continued with a few additions. One addition we treasured was a large red felt advent calendar with a green Christmas tree and twenty-four pockets below the tree. Each pocket held an ornament, elaborately decorated with sequins and beads and a scripture. Each day beginning December 1, we would take one ornament from the pocket, read, and discuss the scripture. The pocket on December 24 held the star that would top the tree. The tree was now complete, which meant the next day was Jesus's birthday. We had a "Happy Birthday, Jesus" cake and celebrated the reason for the season. Gifts and toys were secondary.

All these things are reminders that this is a season for loving and giving. Remember the precious gift God gave us as you remember to bless others as you celebrate the season. Know that He (Jesus) and only He will give you peace, joy, hope, and rest.

Thank you, God, for including me in your plans to bless others and share your gospel.

# Corona: Facing the Facts

The coronavirus hit the world full force in the year 2020 and became a catastrophic pandemic. How did this happen? Did our leaders fail us?

Thinking about how this virus has invoked fear across the nation, is reminiscent of the biblical story of David and Goliath found in 1 Samuel. The Philistines and the giant Goliath had the Israelites terrified. The Coronavirus appears to be much like the Philistines and the giant Goliath that the Israelites were up against. But along came David, a small youth, and took care of the huge problem. Where is our David?

The Israelite leaders feared Goliath from the standpoint that he was too big for them to handle. David had the attitude and fortitude of; he is too big to miss. Many today see only hopelessness at these difficult times—neglecting to see the reality of God's power to bring us through what seems to be an almost impossible situation—much like the Israelites fear of the Philistines.

God has promised to never leave us or forsake us, so what do we do—look around and be distressed, look within and be depressed, or look to Jesus and be at rest? I choose the latter. Look to Jesus. Focus on Him instead of the circumstances of Corona. We need to fill our minds with God's word and concentrate our attention on His promises. Have faith and face reality. Yes, Corona can be deadly. We must use wisdom and take precautions. Each of us must make a conscious effort to try and protect ourselves and those with whom we have contact. But we also must make a conscious choice to believe and trust God, and practice a radical reliance on Him who has the whole world in His care and capable hands. Stand on His promises.

"So do not fear, for I am with you; do not be dismayed, for I am your God. I will strengthen you and help you; I will uphold you with my righteous right hand" (Isaiah 41:10).

Take this attitude: The pandemic was a most definite reminder that we all have a social responsibility. In this case, it was to wear masks and practice safe distancing. Protect yourself and those you have contact with. Read Matthew 25:31–46 and you will find confirmation that it is not just about me. It is about all of us.

# Creating Change

When the pandemic within a pandemic occurred in 2020, local media provided an excellent strong coverage around the "Create Change" movement for several weeks. The photos, the editorials, and the articles about "creating change" really help to promote awareness to the movement. Several of the churches have joined for a twenty-one-day fast and prayer for positive changes to our community. Twenty-one days may seem like an impossible challenge; however, prayer and reading the Word makes it rather easy! And the outcome makes it worth the challenge!

Being part of a family that is sincerely devoted and committed to creating change is a wonderful, heartwarming experience. It makes you feel alive and gives you hope for a better tomorrow.

Most times fasting pertains to food—for example, not eating from 6:00 AM–6:00 PM. Staying hydrated during the day and *ENJOYING a balanced meal* at 6:00 PM. When six o'clock rolls around, you are ready to sit down, thank God, and enjoy your meal! Fasting, praying, and denying your body food, works wonders and leaves you with a clean, bright spirit and appositive outlook for what the future holds.

But food is not the only way to fast. One of my friends was accustomed to playing five computer games of solitaire every day and she decided to abstain from that habit for the twenty-one days. That is her fast. I say good for her. Others have chosen to give up other things. The key is being disciplined enough to deny yourself *and* take the time to faithfully pray.

I am convinced that a fast of "words" would greatly benefit many, many folk—those on the receiving end and those doing the giving. Emily Dickinson once said, "I know nothing in the world that has as much power as a word." Words can destroy more readily than bricks, bombs, or poison. Words can also build up. They can soothe and heal more readily than oil or aloe. Words have so much power.

Growing up, it was common to hear the adage, "Sticks and stones may break my bones, but names will never hurt me." What a falsehood! That was before email and Facebook!

Think about how many lives have been ruined by words or the misuse of words. How many reputations have been tarnished by words? In our modern world, with all the advanced technology, email or posting on social media sites can cause great harm. Words travel fast and can go so many places in almost an instant. The wrong words can be fatal. We have witnessed the devastating effect of "bullying" and the increase in teen suicides—most often because of words. When things go viral, it's often too late for a retraction.

From the very beginning, too many babies and toddlers only hear the words *stop, no, do not, bad.* Not only are the words crushing, but also the tones are often harsh! Misuse of words can lead us to harm others even when we do not realize it.

Job tells us, "Your own mouth condemns you…your own lips testify against you."

Not every word that crosses your mind need be spoken. What comes out of the mouth is a good indication of your heart and your character. David prayed, "Take control of what I say, O Lord, and guard my lips." Perhaps it is easier for us to just say, "Zip my lips." He can help us control what we say. He can guard our lips.

Fasting words will keep us from angry outbursts and demeaning comments, and it will help you control your thoughts. You have a choice whether to say those words or commit them to Him to control. If you slip, do not beat yourself up, just offer those thoughts and words to the Lord, and ask Him to change your thoughts and mind with His character!

In James 3:8, we are told about the toxicity of words, "No human being can tame the tongue. It is a restless evil, full of deadly poison." But in Psalms 39:1, King David resolved, "I will watch my ways and keep my tongue from sin: I will put a muzzle on my mouth." Fast and ask the Lord to do the same for you!

Ask yourself these questions: How have I experienced the power of words in my personal life? Have I ever used words to destroy? Have I ever used words to build up? The answers to these questions will let you know if fasting words is for you!

# Custom-Made

*I*n our society, most people view custom-made items as a sign of prestige and being wealthy. Custom-made drapes are beautiful and expensive and may often be just the touch your home needs to be a showcase. Custom-made suits are "dapper" and show just how stylish one might be. Designer or custom-made wedding gowns, prom gowns, etc., are other examples of crazes to which we succumb. Then there are those who spend many hours and a fortune customizing vintage cars. The whole idea is to have something "special," something out of the ordinary. This is all good.

As a seamstress, I often get requests for custom-made items. What can be done with "scraps," a little planning and some time and patience is amazing. Working with my hands relaxes me and helps me to stay focused on positive things. The creative abilities given to me, are not only a blessing, but they also provide encouragement and personal satisfaction. To recycle or take remnants and make an item that will be used, treasured, and loved by someone brings me joy. Many times, customers prefer to have unique, one-of-a-kind designs for themselves, their pets—yes, pets, or special occasion gifts. These requests sometime present a challenge, but the joy comes from being able to start from "scratch," make something, look at the finished product, and know that it is "good."

Much like my custom-made crafts, each one of us is a unique and special creation. God did not have a "mold" only for certain folks and the rest of us just happened. Each one of us is special in His sight. We are individually made, gifted, and **loved unconditionally**. God gave each of us gifts and talents that we might glorify Him. He designed us just the way He wanted us to be. Yes, we may have made a choice that caused us to deviate from His will—BUT He does allow and "gracefully" accepts U-turns. We must make the effort and take the time to learn what our gifts and talents are and use them. Do not be envious of what someone else does or can do. Your gifts are different from mine because He has a different purpose and job for you to do. He has a different audience for you to reach and different places for you to go. We must learn to play with the hand we were dealt. Do the best we can with what we have and be the best we can be at whatever He has called us to be. This is success.

Booker T. Washington said, "Success is to be measured not so much by the position that one has reached in life as by the obstacles which one has overcome while trying to succeed." So be on your way to success. Be happy and find joy in knowing that you are different, UNIQUE, special, and individually designed—**custom-made**—and that is all **good**! "I praise you because I am fearfully and wonderfully made: your works are wonderful…" (Psalms 139:14).

# Defining Moments

You are the one and only ever you.

—Nancy Tillman

While reading, I came across the above quote, reminding me of how special and unique each one of us are. Embracing our own uniqueness does not necessarily come easily for all of us. What makes each of us uniquely special is not only our personality, essence, or aura, but it is our path and our journey. The path that we take shapes who we are…defining moments mold or character and our being. A car accident, a tragic death, high school or college graduation, marriage, lessons learned, people we meet, and decisions that we make all can be defining moments. How we let these moments touch us can define us. Nancy Tillman's quote brought to mind, "Everything was created by God for God" (Colossians 1:16). Therefore, we know that we all have a purpose. From the time we were conceived, God had something special in mind for each of us. Even though we may not know what that purpose is, our path can help us learn to fulfill our destiny. Each defining moment leads us to who we are supposed to be. Something He wanted us to do and someone He wanted us to be.

Questions. Defining moments! Are you accomplishing this plan? Are you doing things that matter? Are you positively influencing someone's life? Are you showing love? Are you having fun—enjoying life? Are you doing His will?

It is always amazing how a quote, a song, or perhaps even an incident can trigger thoughts that take you to a place of remembrance, deliberation, regret, or perhaps conviction. A defining moment—a time to define and evaluate and appreciate YOU and your gift or gifts.

While reading Nancy Tillman's quote served as a reminder that each of us has a purpose and a special job to do, the lyrics to the song below *confirms* it all!

> You thought I was worth saving
> So, You came in and changed my life
> You thought I was worth keeping
> So, You cleaned me up inside
> You thought I was to die for
> So, You sacrificed your life
> So, I could be free
> So, I could be whole
> So, I could tell everyone I know
> Hallelujah
> Glory to God who changed my life
> I will praise You, forever
> I will worship You, forever
> I will give You glory, forever
> I will give You glory, forever
> Because You deserve it, Lord
> I will praise You, forever

Ponder over those defining moments and watch how you grow, serve, and prosper.

# Detours

When I hear the word *detour*, I immediately get a visual of a large, orange diamond-shaped highway sign that is going to add unplanned time to the trip and change my estimated time of arrival. A nuisance! The alternate route is usually a roundabout way, most often involving back roads, narrow streets, and additional time. However, if you stay on course and follow instructions, you eventually get where you wanted to go.

One of the dictionary definitions for *detour* is "a deviation from a direct course of action." Is that not the path of life? If you seriously think about life's journey, I believe you will have to conclude that life itself is a series of detours. Sometimes the detour is a little "bump," but sometimes it is a "manhole."

The Israelites went through slavery, desert wanderings, rebuilding their homeland, enduring attacks from foreign armies before the dedication of the temple in Jerusalem. Major detours! All these trials and their ultimate survival assured them that God was not absent from their lives.

As it is with each of us, detours may take us where we do not want to go, but if we keep the faith and hold to "God's unchanging hand," we will get to where He wants us to be.

You may enter a relationship with all intentions that it will be forever; however, any number of detours may surface. There could be divorce or even death. Hold on and keep going. God is there bringing you yet closer to Him.

Disease may enter your body. Pray and claim your healing. This detour may be short or long but know that detours are not always bad and look for the positive outcome. Be thankful for each day and each blessing, knowing that God is not absent.

I was involved in an automobile accident that certainly caused a detour in my day, my travels, and my life. True to His Word, God was not absent and took care of all my needs, protecting me from harm and leading me through all that was necessary. This was when I became certain that He is my rock!

Detours take us where we need to go. Sometimes they are burdensome. Sometimes they are educational. Sometimes they are "self-perpetuated." Sometimes the detours make no sense to us. Nevertheless, detours are a part of our lives and many times they are necessary to get us to where God wants us to be. Detours are not just orange traffic signs. Detours get us through life and many times save our lives!

"And we know that in all things God works for the good of those who love Him, who have been called according to His purpose" (Romans 8:28). That even applies to detours!

# Dig a Little Deeper

*I*n preparation for an outstanding year, our church family normally begins the year with twenty-one days of fasting and prayer. Pastor thoughtfully prepares a reading guide and a weekly prayer focus guide. Reading through this outline and the scripture references stirred a desire to expand my reading and "dig deeper." This started somewhat of a chain reaction.

First, I had an embarrassing flashback from my childhood. Growing up, we lived next door to an uncle who was an evangelist in the Church of God. Frequently, he would take me with him, as he travelled to the different churches. I was about eight years old and had recently started piano lessons. I immediately learned and memorized a few of his favorite songs. Consequently, before preaching, he would always have me play a song—usually it was, "Nobody Knows the Trouble I've seen." On one occasion, my younger sister had travelled with us—usually she stayed at home. After I played my song, sibling rivalry surfaced, and she stood up and said, "Can I testify?" The elders quickly responded, "Go ahead, baby." She immediately began clapping and singing, "Dig a little deeper in the storehouse, Lord." I am not sure singing is the right word, because she could not carry a tune if you put it in a bucket. The sight of that little green dress was swaying above the skinny legs, the hand clapping the off-key singing, still flashes vividly in my mind! We laugh about it now, but at the time, it was sheer embarrassment for me!

Second, sometime in 2016, I purchased a 2017 devotional and put it aside. When I retrieved the devotional on January 1 and opened it, the focus for 2017 was "digging deeper." Unintentionally or possible intentionally my focus continued to be connected to digging deeper.

Third, a friend gave me a book, *21-day Journal to a new you.* This devotional includes scriptures, prayers, fitness hints, and journaling. Neat! Again, encouraging me to dig deeper for clarity, growth, and overall wellness.

All of these things combined—church emphasis, daily devotional, and the journal, confirm that the right track for me in 2017 was to dig deeper. Fortunately, I have lived long enough to appreciate and know the difference between knowledge (knowing facts) and wisdom (applying those facts to life). Without wisdom, knowledge is useless.

I began a new routine of daily morning devotions and prayer— first things first. Starting the day by digging deeper into the Word opened new doors of understanding and strengthened me. This was the beginning of my purposeful journey to "dig a little deeper."

"And we know that all things work together for good to them that love God, to them who are called according to His purpose" (Romans 8:28).

# Don't Quit; Press On

*M*ost of us have gone through periods in our life when we feel like throwing in the towel and calling it quits. These are times when we may struggle with feeling all alone and like no one could possibly understand. But there is a still quiet voice telling you, "Do not quit—not yet." So you press on.

You may be going through a tough time in your marriage, and divorce looks like the only way out. Again, there is a presence telling you. Do not give up yet. Press on.

The job is miserable. No one is cooperating, and there seems to be no team players. Everyone is on a solo campaign looking out only for self. What do you do? Look for another job? Join the crowd and become self-centered like the rest of the group? Will the grass be greener on the other side? "Rejoice in the Lord always. Let your gentleness be evident to all. The Lord is near. Do not be anxious about anything, but in everything, by prayer and petition, with thanksgiving, present your requests to God. And the peace of God which transcends all understanding will guard your hearts and your minds in Christ Jesus" (Philippians 4:4–7). Do not quit. Press on.

You get a disturbing medical report. It seems like too much to handle. There are decisions to make about your treatment, future care, finances, etc.… This is the perfect time to cast **all** your cares on the One who promised to never leave you nor forsake you. Grab hold of that promise and press on.

Recently, a dear friend passed on, and she will be greatly missed. She was known by all as a strong-willed fighter. Along this journey of life, she fought a tough battle for years. She endured, impressively, many punches that would have been a TKO for so many of us. However, she had that wonderful wisdom and fighting spirit to press on. When the punches and blows struck, her comment was, "I just have to roll with the punches." In twenty-five years, I never heard her question, "Why me?" Her faith and spirit were admirable. She kept the faith, continued to believe and trust in God. She personified Hebrews 10:35–36. "So do not throw away your confidence; it will be richly rewarded. You need to persevere so that when you have done the will of God, you will receive what he has promised."

Cancer, chemo, radiation, and pain played havoc with her body for many years, but hallelujah, they did not destroy her spirit or faith. While pain was obvious, stronger was her will to endure, press on, and roll with the punches. She loved and enjoyed life.

There is no doubt that her family, friends, and associates knew she firmly believed, "We are not of those who shrink back and are destroyed, but of those who believe and are saved" (Hebrews 10:39). She left an indelible mark on many lives, including mine.

My friend was in a situation where she fed her faith and let doubts and fears starve to death. She rolled with the punches and faithfully pressed on until she received that call to "come home."

So if you are in one of those seemingly unbearable situations, get connected to the Vine. "Seek first his kingdom and righteousness… Don't worry about tomorrow, for tomorrow will worry about itself" (Matthew 6:33–34). "According to your faith will it be done to you" (Matthew 9:29).

Keep the faith and hold to God's unchanging hand.

# Do We Embrace a Culture of Greed?

The dictionary defines greed as an excessive desire to acquire or possess—wealth, power, etc.—beyond what one needs or deserves. That "etc." could be food—one of the things on most folks mind and plates during this holiday season. Many of us will undoubtedly consume and enjoy more food and drink than our body needs. It seems to be an expectation that there be an abundance and variety of foods to celebrate the Thanksgiving holiday. Is that greed?

The biblical definition of greed is quite expansive. Greed is defined as grasping, craving, covetous, desirous, devouring, gluttonous, indulgent, mercenary, miserly, piggish, voracious. Greed accumulates far beyond need. Greed is self-centered and selfish. It lives at the opposite end of the spectrum from generosity, giving, and graciousness. "They are dogs with mighty appetites; they never have enough. They are shepherds who lack understanding; they all turn to their own way; each seeks his own gain" (Isaiah 56:11).

Greed makes us ignorant of others needs and causes us only to think of self. Greed can also overpower us, moving us to covet or go after things we know we should not have. A perfect example of this can be found in 2 Samuel chapters 11 and 12.

Think about this: The homes of the early settlers had no closets. Later, a home built in the early 1900s had one closet, which was approximately three feet wide and about twelve to eighteen inches deep. Moreover, this humble storage was sufficient for the family needs. As we began to accumulate more stuff, we graduated to stand alone wardrobes. Next, there were deeper closets. Then we stepped up to walk in closets, and on to storage rooms. Now we have even outgrown home storage and we rent space in offsite storage sheds to store our extra belongings. Are we storing and holding on to things that others might need and could be using? Is that greed? "Watch out! Be on your guard against all kinds of greed; a man's life does not consist in the abundance of his possessions" (Luke 12:15).

Today's society and culture would have us believe that more is better. Often the philosophy is "hold on to what you got." If you are in that place where material possessions are your thing and you are hording possessions, you might want to take a second look at your life and all your possessions. Take a few minutes and read Luke 12:16–34. Lay it aside. Wait a few minutes and read it again. Has your perspective on holding on to possessions changed? How do you define greed? Is society dictating what you embrace?

# Don't Forget Your Key

It seems that the subject of keys keeps taking space in my thoughts. Along with keys comes the song, "When the praises go up, the blessings come down." This was one of the favorite songs sung by the youth choir, which my daughter was a part of several years ago. The youth sang that song with such confidence and vitality that victory just oozed from their voices. It made one really believe that blessings directly poured from Heaven, just like raindrops falling!

Several recent occurrences brought this song and the exuberance of this youth choir from my memory bank. The key being "have faith, praise, and be thankful for all things."

Sometimes life gets so complicated that we begin to worry, and then we try to—unnecessarily—handle things on our own. We forget the key. God really cares! "Praise be to the Lord, to God our Savior, who daily bears our burdens" (Psalms 68:19).

When problems and pressures confront us, we lapse into a state of depression. Why?

When various obstacles get in our path of life, we often forget about the key. Praise and give thanks! This key turns defeat into victory.

Scriptures tell us that Paul and Silas were sitting in a Philippian jail. They began singing praises, a mighty earthquake came, and the prison doors opened. Not only were they set free, but also the jailer was even converted. (Acts 16:25–36).

2 Chronicles 20:20–25 tells how Jehoshaphat, king of Judah, used the key. He appointed men to sing to the Lord and to praise him for the splendor of his holiness as they went out at the head of the army, saying, "Give thanks to the Lord, for his love endures

forever. As the men begin to sing and praise, the Lord set ambushes against those invading Judah…and they were defeated."

Claim your place knowing that "The Lord is my Shepherd…" (Psalms 23).

"The Lord is my strength and my shield, my heart trusts in Him, and I am helped. My heart leaps for joy and I will give thanks to him in song" (Psalms 28:7).

Remembering to use the key takes faith. Stand firm and use it with confidence. You will be amazed at how the blessings flow. Try it and see for yourself.

# Don't Judge a Book by Its Cover

There he is—tall, dark, handsome, and dressed to perfection. His shoes are shined and unbelievably, he is staring at you. What you do not see is a heart of stone and total immoral character.

Wow! You cannot stop looking at her. The long, wavy hair, long, smooth legs, and body shaped like a Coca-Cola bottle mesmerizes you. She is also flashing the prettiest white teeth ever. Is she really smiling at me? She certainly is! She is on the prey—looking for a "sugar daddy."

You are "house hunting. "The description and the pictures in the real estate magazine present a dream house. The price seems to be a real bargain—first red flag! You are ecstatic to find something within your price range and you are ready to make an offer without even a walk through! However, further research reveals the house is in a flood zone, has been flooded five times or more, and all the "new decorations" are because of a recent flood. The attractive eye-catching decorations are of the cheapest materials possible.

He is sitting alone in the restaurant. The neatly pressed jeans and plaid shirt do not appeal to you. He speaks pleasantly as you walk by—only to be ignored. So happens, he is a sincere, thoughtful, lonely Christian man and could possibly be exactly what God has planned for you.

There is a wise saying, "Before you buy a book, read the foreword." In other words, take some time before you make a choice. Why are we so quick to assume and react without taking the time to pray? We waste so much precious time, energy, and money when we let emotions control our actions. If you are told, you need major surgery or even major house repairs, would you not at least consider getting a second opinion? I know I would. However, when our emotions and intimate decisions are fore front, we quite often "jump" with the quickness, making a mistake that could, and often does, turn our whole world upside down. How much easier life could be if only we would take time—not just to pray—but to also listen! The scriptures tell us, "Be still and know that I am God." What would it hurt to take time to pray, and then wait for an answer?

Food for thought: "All that glitters ain't gold." After all, a manufactured cubic zircon gem looks beautiful, but its value is nothing compared to a "real" diamond. Try not to be in such a hurry that you do not take the time to pray, listen, and "check the foreword."

"Charm is deceptive, and beauty is fleeting; but a woman who fears the LORD is to be praised" (Proverbs 31:30).

And above all, remember: "All that glitters is not gold."

# Dress for Success: The Perfect Outfit

*M*any are familiar with the organization that takes used clothing and recycles to women just joining the workforce or interviewing for jobs. It is important that they make a good appearance. So there are mentors that help them select the appropriate attire for their situation. They are attempting to dress for success—looking for that perfect outfit.

We have all had a meeting or special occasion to attend, where we believed it was crucial to be properly attired. These occasions make us anxious and often cause us unnecessary stress.

Often, we go to any length to either purchase a new outfit, borrow an outfit or accessory from a friend, or thoroughly search through our closets for that perfect piece to tie it all together. We spend time and put a lot of effort on our outward appearance, which can easily be changed by a sudden rainfall, a slip, or fall in the mud, or something as simple as being splashed by a passing vehicle while crossing the street.

Using God's clothes closet eliminates the stress and anxiety and gives us the perfect outfit for any occasion.

In Colossians 3:12, Paul specifically advises and reminds us of five wardrobe selections: compassion, kindness, humility, gentleness, and patience. Being that Paul says we can "put on" these qualities, it must mean that we have a choice. Yes, you and I do have a choice as to whether we want the "perfect outfit."

Think about this, when women get dressed, good undergarments make a big difference in how an outfit looks and fits. If you are concerned about your appearance, it is unlikely that you would wear a flimsy sports bra under a knit dress. Undergarments are the foundations to a smooth neat appearance. The same is true for each of us. For daily living, we must also have the right foundation. Choose from God's wardrobe. While it is important to have a good foundation, it still takes the right accessory to pull the outfit together. Colossians 3:14 makes the disclaimer that pulls the clothing from Gods wardrobe into perfect focus. "Put on love, which binds everything together in perfect unity." What does love to have to do with it? Love is the coordinate, that perfect accessory that we were searching for, that pulls it all together. What a pleasing sight to see and what a witness for God, when we have the "perfect outfit."

Once we make the decision to follow Jesus, dressing for success, in that perfect outfit is not difficult.

# Echoes from the Past

*K*udos and thanks to the editors and staff of this newspaper for the article "A sad part of history—but one we should never forget" that appeared in the February 2 edition of the paper. Acknowledging that while strides have been made there is still much to be done, provides hope for some continued progress. Thanks also for the profiles recognizing African Americans in our community that are making great contributions to our society and making this a better place to live. Yes, there have been much advancement since the days of slavery, yet there is still too much hidden bigotry and racism. One glaring example is the movie *Selma* that was only shown in this area for about a week. In addition, while David Oyelowo, the actor that portrayed Dr. King was given raving reviews by the critics for his outstanding performance, Hollywood did not consider him for a Grammy award. It seems that there were no African Americans given that honor or opportunity this year, although there were several that were outstanding. Another example is the Kevin Costner movie *Black and White*. The local theater has been showing the previews for months, it is being advertised on national and local TV networks and the internet shows it to be currently running at our local Cinemark, yet it is not here. We inquired at the theater about the movie and we were told it would probably not be shown here. Driving to Morgantown to see the movie is an option, but somehow that shows complacency. *Black and White* is not the first or only movie dealing with color that our local theater did not provide access to, so maybe it's time to think about not attending any movies there! The newspaper is moving forward and making progress, but the theater seems to be lagging!

Going through some of my files on Black history, I found the following writing that I am going to share...

A very humorous and revealing story is told about a group of white people who were fed up with African Americans, so they joined and wished themselves away. They passé through a deep dark tunnel and emerged in sort of a twilight zone where there is an America without any Black people.

At first, these white people breathed a sigh of relief. At last, they said, no more crime, drugs, violence, and welfare. All the Blacks are gone! Then suddenly reality set in. The "New America" is not America at all, only a barren land.

1.  There are very few crops that have flourished because the nation was built on a slave-supported system.
2.  There are no cities with tall skyscrapers because Alexander Mills, a Black man, invented the elevator, and without it, one finds great difficulty reaching higher floors.
3.  There are few if any cars because Richard Spikes, a Black man, invented the automatic gearshift, Joseph Gambol, also Black, invented the super charge system for the internal combustion engines, and Garrett A. Morgan, a Black man invented traffic signals.
4.  Furthermore, one could not use the rapid transit system because its procurer was the electric trolley, which was invented by another Black man, Albert R. Robinson.
5.  Even if there were streets on which cars and a rapid transit system could operate, they were cluttered with paper because an African American, Charles Brooks, invented the street sweeper.
6.  There were few if any newspapers, magazines, and books because John Love invented the pencil sharpener, William Purveys invented the fountain pen, and Lee Barrage invented the typewriting machine and W. A. Love invented the advanced printing press. They were all, you guessed it, Black.

7. Even if Americans could write their letters, articles, and books, they would not have been transported by mail because William Barry invented the postmarking and cancelling machine. William Purveys invented the hand stamp and Phillip Downing invented the letter drop.

8. The lawns were brown and wilted because Joseph Smith invented the lawn sprinkler and John Burr the lawn mower.

9. When they entered their homes, they found them to be poorly ventilated and poorly heated. You see, Frederick Jones invented the air conditioner and Alice Parker the heating furnace. Their homes were also dim. But of course, Lewis Lattimore later invented the lantern, and Granville T. Woods invented the automatic cut off switch. Their homes were also filthy because Thomas W. Stewart invented the mop, and Lloyd P. Ray the dustpan.

10. Their children met them at the door bare-footed, shabby, motley, and unkempt. But what could one expect? Jan E. Matzeliger invented the shoe lasting machine, Walter Sammons invented the comb, Sarah Boone invented the ironing board, and George T. Samon invented the clothes dryer.

11. Finally, they were resigned to at least have dinner amidst all of this turmoil. But here again, the food had spoiled because another Black man, John Standard invented the refrigerator.

Now, isn't that something? What would this country be like without the contributions of Blacks, as African Americans?

Martin Luther King Jr. said, "By the time we leave for work, Americans have depended on the inventions from the minds of Blacks."

Black history includes more than just slavery, Frederick Douglass, Martin Luther King Jr., Malcom X, Marcus Garvey, and W. E. B. Dubois.

Good news: "The body is not made up of one part, but many" (1 Corinthians 12:14).

These little nuggets are just a snack—some food for thought!

# Embrace Rest

$\mathcal{S}$ pring is here! All around us, we see signs of new life, new growth, and new beginnings. Much of what we witness and are enjoying is the result of winter's rest and deep nourishment. All of spring's bright and beautiful display comes from the wonderful balance created by nature—nutrients from the soil, sunshine, and heat from the air, and moisture from the heavens. Magnificent!

Most of us are familiar with the term R&R. To some it may mean rest and relaxation. I propose that we think recovery and restoration. It is no secret that we all need balance in our lives. Too often, we work, work, work, run, run, run, and leave little or no time for rest. Guilty?

A dear friend, who passed a few years ago, often tried to persuade me to take at least one day every two weeks and do nothing. She advocated that I should stay in PJs and robe all day, and just lounge, read a book, watch TV, or whatever took me to that "happy place" of comfort. At the time, I did not think that was a possibility—I had too much I wanted to do. Since her passing, I have not only indulged in that philosophy, but I have also learned to appreciate and enjoy this newfound way of relaxing.

Since everyone is unique, everyone must establish what constitutes rest for him or her. Look at the things you contribute to the world through your relationships, your creativity, your heart, your words, and your hands. These are the things that you own and make you unique. They refuel your soul and give you life. Much like what happens to nature over the winter.

Embracing rest may mean relearning what your needs are. Rest does not necessarily mean curling up on the sofa with a good book and a cup of tea or glass of wine, silence, or the overrated, in my opinion, power nap. It is finding practices or things that help you own the now. Embracing rest daily could be something as simple as chair time—curling up in your favorite chair with your pet or doing some stretches. On a weekly basis, consider creating something—a collage, a garden, meeting with an on-going group of some kind. Find something that you really enjoy. For monthly restoration, visit a friend, or perhaps take a short trip. For a quarterly restoration: you may want to consider attending a creative workshop—something that would enhance one of your hobbies. For annual restoration: a retreat, a getaway with friends or spouse/partner.

A vacation or trip to the beach always restores me. Getting away from all the hustle and bustle of life's daily activities, chores that need done, requests for time is a real treat and allows for restoration and recovery.

Think about things in your life that will help you return to you! Know that some of the deepest and most beautiful parts of us go dormant during certain seasons of life and we must make the effort to wake them back up. Let us learn to put our efforts and intentions toward things that give life—things that put a sparkle in your eyes and wonder in your heart.

It is up to You to define the balance between rest and work. Keep the pendulum swinging in balance and you will be able to sincerely state, "I have learned the secret of being content in any and every situation…" Embrace rest!

# Every Day Matters

*H*ow did you spend yesterday? Did you do or say something to someone that made a difference in their life? Do you recall what you did to please God? How will you spend today? Will what you do or say matter to someone? What can you do or say to help or comfort someone? Remember, every day matters!

Think of each day much like a trip to a cafeteria—a huge smorgasbord. The sights are appealing. As you proceed through the line, there are so many choices. We are hungry and there are many selections and appealing temptations in front of us. You know the pit falls of some of the choices and you also know you have decisions to make. This cafeteria is not one where everyone pays the same price, and you can eat all you want. It is one of those places where you make your choices and pay at the end of the line. Your choices matter, physically, mentally, and financially. The choices immediately determine the impact on your funds; however, the physical and mental impact may be a little delayed. Before you are the options of a healthy protein, cooked vegetables, fresh garden salad, mouthwatering carbs of all kinds, and a variety of almost irresistible desserts, plus a variety of drink choices. The choices are yours to make. Each item on that tray is at a cost-much like the choices before us each day of our lives. Every choice matters, like every day matters.

Today matters. The time is now. Take some time today to pray. Pray that you will do His will. Pray for the sick and homeless. Pray for this country of ours that is so tied up and tangled up in sin and unrest. Take some time to read and study His Word. Take some time to do some good for your neighbor or for your community. Send some love to someone by way of a card, a phone call, or a text. Let someone know that they matter. Just reach out! Every day matters.

Maya Angelou once said, "I've learned that no matter what happens, or how bad it seems today, life goes on, and it will be better tomorrow." So if you feel you let today slip by, do better tomorrow.

On this journey through life, the choices we make cost greatly or reward us in the end. "Whatever you do in word or deed, do all in the name of the Lord Jesus, giving thanks to God the Father through Him" (Colossians 3:17).

What you do or do not accomplish is all recorded on that dash between DOB and DOD (date of birth and date of death). What will be recorded on your dash?

# Facts of Life

Looking back over some of my previous writings, I realized that while the topics were given to me as a ministry to perhaps help others, they have sustained and encouraged me. Life situations allowed me to make a pitcher of lemonade from all the lemons given to me. Multiple detours took me totally by surprise; nevertheless, following the course, the detours are slowly bringing my life back to some normalcy. In the blink of an eye, my car was totaled, but I was protected and remained safe and unharmed! To me, this is factual evidence that it is not who we are, but whose we are!

While going through these storms, a friend shared the following story. It helped me, and I am hoping it touches your heart also.

At birth, we boarded the train and met our parents, and we believe they will always travel by our side. However, at some station our parents will step down from the train, leaving us on this journey alone.

As time goes by, other people will board the train, and they will be significant—our siblings, friends, children, and even the love of your life.

Many will step down and leave a permanent vacuum. Others will go so unnoticed that we do not realize they vacated their seats.

This train ride will be full of joy, sorrow, fantasy, expectations, hellos, goodbyes, and farewells.

Success consists of having a good relationship with all passengers, requiring that we give the best of ourselves.

The mystery to everyone is—we do not know at which station we ourselves will step down. Therefore, we must live in the best way, love, forgive, and offer the best of who we are. It is important to do this because when the time comes for us to step down and leave our seat empty; we should leave behind beautiful memories for those who will continue to travel on the train of life.

"So, you must be ready, because the Son of Man will come at an hour when you do not expect Him" (Matthew 24:44).

I wish you a joyful journey on the train of life. Reap success and give lots of love. More importantly, thank God for the journey.

Lastly, I thank you for being one of the passengers on my train. By the way, I am not planning to get off the train anytime soon, but if I do, just remember I am glad you were part of my journey, and I am thankful for the journey.

# Fake News

*L*ately we have been hearing a lot about "fake news" and all the politically bias reports.

Think about how the news reports and the information that spreads so rapidly through the media influences you and your daily living. Has all the reporting and scandalous surprises changed your viewing perspectives? Previously, you may have religiously watched CNN or FOX to stay aware of what was happening in the world. Do you now feel confident that all the reporting is factual? I know of many who have stopped watching the national news channels because of all the foolishness.

Do you ever wonder what percentage of our population relies on the TV, the internet, and Facebook for news and/or tips on daily living? My response to that question would be—too many!

By watching TV, following Facebook, and Googling you can get all kinds of information and advice on how to lose those extra pounds, how to manage your money, how to reduce or deal with stress, how to manage relationships, how to live longer, how to be happy, and the list continues. All this information comes from experts in their field. Much of the information is only a "teaser," and to get the "real deal" you must spend your hard-earned dollars and make purchase. Is this information you can rely on? Do you have any guarantee that this information will solve your problem? Will this media advice give you temporary or permanent relief?

It is getting harder to find God in our modern technology world but try this theory. You will only need to go to one resource—the B-I-B-L-E. "Your word is a lamp for my feet and a light for my path" (Psalm 119:105).

**Eliminate debt**: "Let no debt remain outstanding, except the continuing debt to love one another" (Romans 13:8). When we were growing up, my father would not make any purchase that he could not pay cash for. I have remembrances of hearing my parents discuss the need for a new refrigerator. Mom wanted the refrigerator now, and she was trying to convince Daddy to open an account at Sears and make monthly payments. She did not win. Daddy's argument was that, if anything happened to him, he loved us too much to leave us with debt. This philosophy greatly influenced me. And to this day, although I use my credit cards, I only make purchases that I can pay off before the next billing cycle!

**Reduce stress**: "And the peace of God which transcends all understanding, will guard your hearts and mind in Christ Jesus" (Philippians 4:7).

**Healthful eating**: "So whatever you eat or drink or whatever you do, do it for the glory of God" (1 Corinthians 10:31).

**Improve your love life**: "Love is patient, love is kind. It does not envy, it does not boast, it is not proud" (1 Corinthians 13:4).

**To live longer**: "If you walk in obedience to me and keep my decrees...I will give you a long life" (1 Kings 3:14).

**Be prosperous**: "Bring all the tithes into the storehouse...If you do, I will open the windows of heaven for you. I will pour out a blessing so great you will not have room to take it in! Try it! Let me prove it to you!" (Malachi 3:10).

Tired of fake news? Click through the WORD and there you will find the best, honest, and true counseling, and advice. Read Exodus 23:22–25.

# February Celebrations

$\mathcal{T}$he month begins with Pennsylvania Punxsutawney Phil, and West Virginia Freddie casting their weather predictions for our winter life. Looks like we play the wait and see game to validate their predictions! However, their sighting always gives us something to look forward to coming February 1.

We also have Valentine's Day, and the purchase of candy, flowers, and diamonds as expressions of love. The stores are enticingly decorated with red hearts, red roses, beautiful greeting card displays, and signs suggesting/recommending potential love gifts. Florists gear up for the many deliveries and special floral arrangements. Restaurants also offer specials for the romantic dinners for two! Love is in the air—as it should be!

President's Day also falls in this month. For many, this is a paid holiday from work and for others an opportunity to take advantage of the many sales being offered.

Wow! Not just a day, but the whole month of February is designated, Black History Month. Another year has passed since some of us are thinking about and talking about Black History and the contributions made by our Black ancestors to our American way of life. The entire month of February is dedicated to celebrating, recognizing, and even honoring "Black" contributions to American society. Many things that were omitted and left out of the "American" history books are now being talked about. Some of the local organizations, churches, schools, and universities are planning special programs, bringing in guest speakers or holding some type of program recognizing Black contributions. Others are simply doing nothing!

The recent movie *Hidden Figures* is a primary example of a well-kept educational secret. When all the happenings and excitement took place around the moon launching, was there ever a Black face in those pictures? Just think how motivating it would have been for a struggling student to have witnessed a person of color being involved with the moon mission. That one example of a Black mathematician could have given so many hope for a brighter future. Now that the book is available and the movie is showing, a teachable opportunity presents itself. Having a meeting, discussing, and sharing about life during that period could be a very positive learning experience—for both the youth and the adults. In addition, the separate, but equal philosophy needs to be explained to our youth, so they will know and more importantly appreciate the advances that have been made—in some areas!

Black History—yes, as we look back, we see the many positive changes, and many continue to have faith and hope that things will continue to move forward. Many see the positive outcome of the struggles, the marches, the peaceful protests, and the relentless prayers. Yet there are thousands, perhaps millions, of Black and Brown people who dreadfully fear their future. There is fear and anxiety regarding deportation and separation of families. There is fear and anxiety about healthcare, clean water, and even public education. Then there is "The Wall."

Where are we headed? Are we back to focusing and leaning on the Negro National Anthem, "We shall overcome, someday..."?

My recommendation is to concentrate on the scriptures. "You are all sons of God through faith in Christ Jesus" (Galatians 3:26).

# Focus on the 80 Not the 20

*I*f you take an exam and get an 80 percent, you at least passed. Eighty percent was not the grade you wanted, but it is better than being the reverse. A grade of 20 percent would be devastating! So the focus should be on trying to improve the 80!

Studies show that marriages often dissolve because one person feels they are missing something in the relationship. Usually this is something small that is blown out of proportion. Then, after much heartache and confusion, reality sets in and one finds that the grass is not greener on the other side of the street! Someone concentrated on the 20 instead of the 80.

A young Black man commits a violent crime. Consequently, every time you see a young Black man nearby, you lock your car doors, hold tightly to your purse and cringe in fear. Once again, the focus is on the 20, but the 80 suffer the consequences.

Recently the forces of evil have taken center stage in our country. The ugly head of prejudice and violence is once again being displayed openly and proudly. The media follow the events and the perpetrators vividly and closely, helping to stir up unrest and fear for many. While only a small percent of our population constitutes those causing the conflict and disturbances, it appears massive. We must not allow the 20 to discourage us and lose faith. It is imperative that we focus on the 80! Read and study Psalms 37.

Do not fall prey to letting the performance of one or a few discourage you. Continue to extend love and kindness whenever you have the opportunity. If we want things to be different and if we want change, it must begin within each of us. Put the right things in your heart and mind and then move forward. We cannot change the past, but we can be thankful that it is the past. Since we are in the present, we can participate in making it better. Do your part to make peace and do God's will. The future is in God's hands, so know that He is in control and will work it out!

Yes, evil is very visible, but I believe, and I hope you do too, that there are heavenly forces working behind the scenes, and that this too will pass! (Psalms 44:1–8).

# Follow the Instructions

*H*ave you ever purchased a DIY (do-it-yourself) project, and thought, this looks easy; I will have it done in no time? Two days later, you still have an incomplete mess!

How much time and energy we would save if we would only learn to follow instructions. Our stress levels would be less, and those around us would be happier, if we would only follow instructions. However, in the case of DIYs, you must first **READ** the instructions and check to make sure there are no missing or broken parts.

Sad but true, too many of us try to live our lives the same way we tackle a DIY project—without reading the instructions—the Bible. The instruction found in this book truly does provide "basic instructions before leaving Earth."

Think about some of the problems and issues that haunt us individually and affect our society today.

Depression and anxiety, for example, are concerns that might possibly be healed by dwelling on Psalm 100—clear readable instructions for giving thanks and finding joy.

The destructive forces within our communities—violence, hatred, drug abuse, illicit sex—would be less and weakened if we read and followed Proverbs 3:5–6. "Trust in the Lord with all your heart; and lean not unto thy own understanding. In all your ways acknowledge him, and he will direct your paths." Reading and following these instructions to lean on Him—who is always dependable, reliable, and safe—is like having the very best preventive medical care. So many problems would be stopped before things got out of control.

Many of our youth are suffering. Too many are abused, neglected, mistreated, and feel unloved. Did we not read, Proverbs

22:6? "Train up a child in the way he should go; and when he is old, he will not depart from it." How can we possibly train our children if we do not know the way? We must read and study the instructions! We must teach our children to read and follow the instructions. Then they can see for themselves, that they too must be accountable. For the scriptures plainly tells them, "Children obey your parents in the Lord: Honor your father and mother; that it may be well with thee, and that you may enjoy long life on earth" (Ephesians 6:1–3). How else will they know?

How do we face and cope with obstacles put on our paths? One answer can be found in 1 Thessalonians 5:16–18, "Be joyful always. Pray without ceasing. In everything give thanks…" Reading instructions involves and solves much!

For daily living, the instructions found in 1 Corinthians 15:58 and Malachi 3:10 are more than precious and will sustain and cover us thoroughly. Check them out.

Let us take some time and make our plans and to-do lists around the instructions in the greatest book ever written! That will be your key to a more productive, stress-free life.

# Get Moving

t the beginning of each New Year, there is usually much talk about New Year resolutions and goals. The same "old" things seem be on top of the list of resolutions. Many of us vow to lose weight, spend more time at the gym, exercise more, or increase the number of steps we take daily. Others plan to spend more time with the family, make better food choices, or get more involved with helping others. Then there may be some who realize that they should be doing less of something. For instance, less shopping, less drinking, less cursing, less wasting time, etc.

It seems that at the start of a New Year, we are anxious to make positive changes in our lives. Moreover, most of us are energized at the thought of a "new beginning." It so reminds me of 2 Corinthians 5:17: "When anyone is united to Christ, there is a new world; the old order has gone, and a new order has already begun." The start of a new year is like that awakening. Once that ball drops in Times Square, a strange movement occurs. While reflecting on the past, and looking forward to the future, we somehow become extremely vulnerable to making promises and commitments that many of us are, unfortunately, unwilling, or unable to keep. It is much like the excitement that often wears off after first becoming a Christian. Why is that? Could it be that we anticipate change, but fail to move on to change our behaviors?

Thinking back to 1999, the business world was frightfully panicked of moving into the twenty-first century and the potential of computers crashing and all kinds of technical issues with telephones, loss of data, system failures, etc. Technicians were all on alert, prepared to try to handle the possible major problems expected with the decade change to the year 2000. And nothing crashed! There was no major disaster and data converted rather painlessly to the new decade. The scare was all about moving—data and technology. In life, we are destined to keep moving.

What would happen if we all did like it says in Isaiah 60:1, "Rise and shine; for your light has come, and the glory of the Lord has risen upon you..."? Think about it. What would our homes, churches, community, and the world be like, if each one of us would **move**, leap to our potential, sharing and using our unique gifts and talents contributing to society?

Each approaching New Year will not be a pivotal year like 2000 but stop procrastinating! Get moving. Set some "stretch" goals. Use your gifts and talents to the best of your ability. Let your light shine. Follow your dreams! Pursue your passion! Seek God's will for your life. Get moving! Above all, be encouraged to move closer to God.

# Get Your Groove On

You have all heard the saying "There is more than one way to skin a cat." This means there is more than one way to accomplish whatever task or situation one may be facing. If you want to go to Atlanta, you can drive, fly, or get on a bus or train. You have options. If you want to cook a roast, there is the oven, a cast iron roaster on the stovetop, or a slow cooker. If you want to remove the hair from your legs, you might use a razor and shave, or use a depilatory such as Nair, or you could visit a spa and get waxed. You have choices. If you want to read a book, you might choose the iPad version, a hard copy, or even an audio version. You have options! There are many things in life that you have choices to make that will give you the same results. Unfortunately, too many folks take that saying literally and they apply it to important and critical life situations. Think twice before you fall into that mine hole and cannot get out. On the extreme, if you need a kidney transplant, a knee replacement would not be a choice you would pursue.

With each approaching day, consider a fresh start. Really get your groove on.

Start each day with a bang! Resolve to adapt and focus on what you can do to bless someone. If you are already doing that, do more! Make a deliberate decision to do whatever it takes to not just read and study the Bible, but to develop and have a better relationship with the author. If you are not one to make New Year resolutions, try doing the above anyway.

When you step out in faith—trusting, hoping, and believing—with an attitude of giving and loving, you will discover joy, not external happiness but that internal peace and contentment that soothes the soul.

While there may be more than one way to skin a cat, "There is one God, and one mediator between God and men, the man Christ Jesus..." (1 Timothy 2:5).

"Neither is there salvation in any other: for there is none other name under heaven given among men, whereby we must be saved" (Acts 4:12).

Jesus himself said, "I am the way, and the truth and the life. No one comes to the Father except through me" (John 14:6).

You can get your groove on by doing whatever it takes to connect and grow your relationship with our Savior. It only takes a spark to get a fire going. Let the fireworks begin. O happy day!

# God's Ps

*I*f you have ever purchased anything that needs assembled, you recognize the importance of reading and following the instructions. This simple step saves time, helps eliminate stress, and allows you to have a completed project that will usually serve well the purpose for which it is intended. When you "fly by the handle"—go off on your own—and start the project without any guidance, you may have a flop, and much self-created stress. You may also have some extra screws and bolts or pieces that are out of alignment.

Purchasing a new vehicle and just driving it off the lot without instructions or reading the owner's manual opens the door for all kinds of trouble. The keyless vehicles take some knowledge to operate safely. Take heed!

When taking on various projects, or making new purchases, our philosophy is often, the three Ls: live, love, and laugh! This is a temporary fix and may get you through the moment, and any accompanying instructions may seem frivolous!

This journey of life, more importantly than the above examples, has an **owner's** manual (the B-I-B-L-E), that gives us explicit instructions on anything that we might encounter. These are instructions that we must peruse and not skim over. Believe me, it behooves us to not only read, but also study, examine, and apply those instructions to our daily living. Do you know any other manual that provides complete instructions on anything you can possibly think of? This is where and how we encounter **God's Ps—presence, power, promises, and past performance.**

If we look at *Webster's* definitions of the Ps, we find the following:

**Presence:** A supernatural influence felt to be nearby. In actuality, the protective, comforting aura that surrounds you is magical (2 Chronicles7:14, Jeremiah 29:11–13, Revelation 3:20).

**Power:** The ability to act or perform effectively. The Bible tells us of Creation, the Cross, and the Resurrection (Revelation 1:8).

**Promises:** A declaration that one will or will not do something. The Bible is filled with promises that we can depend on. Read Hebrews 10:23.

**Past Performances:** the act or style of performing a work or role. What has God done for you? How has He protected you in the past? How has He provided for you and your loved ones? Where do you think you would be right now without Him?

God loves us. He loves us every single moment, in every possible way, through every circumstance, with all His Heart. Do you love Him enough to rely on and hold fast to God's Ps?

# The Good Old Days

*O*nce again, taking a stroll down memory lane and recalling all the fun and carefree days of my youth (the good old days) makes me so thankful for the parents I had, the community I grew up in and the time of my youth. There were no worries about drugs, meth labs, parents abusing and killing their children, senseless shootings, killing rampages and media exploitation of crimes.

If you had a "beef" with a schoolmate or neighborhood kid, you would threaten to "kick butt" after school; consequently, later there might or might not be a fistfight or "tussle" in the grass. Moreover, if by chance you happened to be careless (stupid) enough to start the ruckus on school property, a paddling took place in the principal's office, followed by additional punishment at home.

In the evenings, before 8:00 p.m.—curfew time—the neighborhood kids would gather for a game of "kick the can." We would play in the street, with our parents sitting on the porch watching as we kicked the can, ran the bases, and giggled.

The can was usually an empty soup can or something similar, and the bases were large stones, stored on the side of the road when they were not bases.

On other occasions, we would play Hopscotch, Simon Says or Jacks. Sometimes we would just shoot marbles.

Cowboys and Indians were great fun. Some of us had cowboy and cowgirl outfits, cowboy hats, cap pistols that made noise, and others had bows and arrows.

We would climb trees, hide behind bushes, or telephone poles and have shootouts. I treasured my Dale Evans outfit, a red skirt and vest with white fringes and a gun holster, and a cap pistol.

What stands out most is that things were always done in groups. People openly communicated and talked to one another. There was sincere conversation, companionship, and creativity.

Kids got exercise—physical and mental—fresh air, and they learned social skills.

Technology is great, but I believe we have overextended its usefulness. Today, too often, technology is our babysitter. Not good!

Our youth are very versed in texting, computer games, iPhone technology, etc., but are missing out on many other things. Many do not like to be outdoors unless it's a sports event. Obesity is the result of lack of exercise. Social skills are suffering. The technology too often is misused and abused.

In the "good old days," there was no addictions to computer games. In fact, we did not have computers.

Telephone call were limited and so was TV watching. Kids were never left alone to watch TV or with some other technology device to keep them occupied. Babysitters or kid sitters was the norm.

Parents were our protectors, our providers, and our motivators. After chores and schoolwork, time was spent doing things with family and or friends.

Board games were a favorite. I remember many evenings playing Monopoly. A Monopoly game would sometimes continue into the next day. To me, Monopoly was often boring, and it was not one of my favorites.

Other pastimes included the Old Maid card game, dominoes, Chinese checkers, checkers, and Rummy. The general rule was that every Christmas we would get a new game.

At about the age of eight, Scrabble came into my world. Wow! What excitement! Scrabble was a fun way to learn new words. It also provided an opportunity to develop strategies and was a fun way to be competitive.

It was not long before Scrabble became my game of choice, and it is still my favorite. Along the way, charades, Scattegories, probe, backgammon, and chess, all had their day, but none so far can outrank Scrabble.

I know time changes things and people, but old is good in some things. The old games kids used to play, old songs, old movies, and old friends. That is nostalgia! And it is good! "We have these treasures in jars of clay..." (2 Corinthians 4:7).

I am still collecting and holding on to different versions of Scrabble boards. "Train a child in the way he should go, and when he is old, he will not depart from it" (Proverbs 22:6).

# Happy Feet?

$\mathcal{D}$o you have happy feet? You may have bunions, flat feet, crooked toes, or hammer toes, but other than this type of uncontrollable physical issue, are your feet pleased with where you have taken them?

Perhaps you have tried to console your feet by soaking and massaging them with softening creams or treating them to pedicures. Did it help?

Think about this. If your feet could see and talk, what would they tell others about the journey they have travelled? Would they be rejoicing, or would they be sad? Would they be thankful for a good cleaning after all the mud? Would they be content?

Life is a journey, and many would agree that the journey could be exciting, beautiful, and even thrilling. It can also be tedious, stressful, and difficult to endure. However, good shoes or good walking boots might make the walk easier. The key though is not the specific foot apparel, but to walk in the light! "There are twelve hours of daylight. A man who walks by day will not stumble, for he sees by this world's light. It is when he walks by night that he stumbles, for he has no light" (John 11:9–10).

In the book of Joshua, Moses told Caleb, "The land on which you walked will be your inheritance and that of your children forever, because you have followed the Lord my God wholeheartedly" (Joshua 14:9). Wow! Has your walk been such that you would want it to be a part of your estate and passed on to your children? That is a claim, I cannot honestly make.

The many references in the scriptures concerning walking and following the "light" to avoid stumbling and falling and taking the "crooked path," confirms my belief that being grounded in the Word, will help keep your feet on solid ground and on the right path. The old cliché "What's done in the dark, will show in the light" has scriptural basis.

Know that there are times that the going may get rough and the path we are on may seem to be leading nowhere. Do not get overwhelmed. Grab the Good Book, read Proverbs 4, look down at your trusty feet and remember they have brought you this far.

Shine those shoes, don a pair of cute sandals or a pair of rocking hot boots, and keep on stepping in the "light." Remember, the journey is to be lived with a song in your heart, a twinkle in your eye and Jesus on your mind! Dance while you can and keep those feet happy!

# Happy Hookers

*T*he context of how words are used can have a crucial impact. I believe the title of this article today may have caught the eyes of a few new readers! Just a thought!

A story is told about the mother of a six-year-old. She was practically begging this kid—when you talk to the neighbors about your aunt, please learn to say that your aunt likes to crochet. Do not call her the "happy hooker."

This past week provided me the opportunity to work with a group of "happy hookers." About a dozen women spent the morning crocheting and knitting scarves for cancer patients. The atmosphere was pleasant, relaxed, and enjoyable. As one of the instructors (facilitator's), we were able to share a few different patterns with the class, coach them on the various stitches, and provide information specifically about the rise of pancreatic cancer. The information sharing also included information about the various colors associated with different kinds of cancer—for example pink for breast and ovarian cancers, lime green for lymphoma, and purple for pancreatic cancer. The goal is to make and accumulate many, many scarves and present them to as many as we can possibly reach. West Virginia Extension Service sponsored this class and several of the attendees are members of local CEOS (Community Education Outreach Services) clubs. If you have any interest is becoming a "happy hooker" or helping with this effort, contact the West Virginia Extension office for additional information. If you are a member of a CEOS group, you might encourage your club to become a part of this initiative. If you just want to participate in the effort as an individual that would also be great. If you do not "hook," you may want to purchase and donate yarn. There are many ways to become involved if you are inclined to participate and be a blessing to someone dealing with this affliction. Another thought is to start your own small group. Meet once a week or once a month and enjoy the company of others while doing something meaningful and working toward making someone else happy.

It has been noted that if you want to be happier, try making your life a little harder. Seriously! Use a push mower. Bake your own bread. Knit or crochet a scarf. Do things by hand and your brain will thank you. It seems that when you do meaningful work with your hands, a kind of neurochemical feedback floods your brain with dopamine and serotonin. These "happy" brain chemicals are natural antidepressants and we have evolved to release them both to reward ourselves for working with our hands and to motivate ourselves to do it some more. So "hooking" is meaningful, rewarding, productive, fulfilling and helps you stay connected. Moreover, Proverbs 11:25 tells us, "He who refreshes others will himself be refreshed." So let us recruit some more "happy hookers."

# Open Mouth, Insert Foot

*I*f we are honest, all of us at some time have said something that caused someone discomfort and maybe even agony. We may have made a comment that was misconstrued or maybe misheard. Since so many of us have selective hearing, it is not difficult to only hear part of what was said, thereby getting the wrong impression. Therefore, listening is just as, if not more important than speaking.

Thinking about how vicious words can be, I searched for some sayings or clichés and accompanying scriptures that might help with keeping your mouth out of trouble.

**"The trouble with the guy who talks too fast is that he often says something he hasn't thought about yet."** Always being on the defensive, ready to answer or snap, before thinking is dangerous. The scriptures tell us, "Do not be quick with your mouth, and do not be hasty in your heart to utter anything before God. God is in heaven and you are on earth, so let your words be few" (Ecclesiastes 5:2). When you do speak, think, and do not make way for opportunities to open your mouth and stick your foot in it!

**"A shut mouth gathers no foot."** If someone shares something very personal with you, value that confidence. Treat it as if they had left their wallet full of money and credit cards on your sofa. Would you take that wallet and give it to someone else? I do not think so. "He who guards his lips guards his life, but he who speaks rashly will come to ruin" (Proverbs 13:3).

**"The only fool bigger than the person who knows it all is the person who argues with him."** As we gain wisdom and mature, we know that there is no point in arguing with a know-it-all person. Better to let them have their say, even if they do have the last word, and walk on. "Whoever corrects a mocker invites insult; whoever rebukes a wicked man incurs abuse" (Proverbs 9:7).

**"Whoever gossips to you will be a gossip of you."** It seems that many fall prey to this trap. If you make it known that you do not want to hear any gossip, people will not attempt to share rumors and such with you. "A talebearer revealed secrets; but he that is of a faithful spirit concealeth the matter" (Proverbs 11:13).

**"A minute of thought is worth an hour of talk."** Before needlessly rambling, breathe. Take time to connect through prayer and think before you speak. Just like David, ask God, "Set a guard over my mouth, O Lord; keep watch over the door of my lips" (Psalms 141:3).

**"You can win more friends with your ears than with your mouth."** Think of a time when you wanted to comfort someone and just could not find the right words. Perhaps a hug was the right communication. "Let every man be swift to hear, slow to speak…" (James 1:19).

**"Never pass up a chance to keep your mouth shut."** Never let yourself be pressured into saying something when you do not feel like talking, or into saying something you don't want to say. Silence is not always a lack of communication. It can be a very effective form of communication. As reminded by Judge Judy, "God gave us two ears and one mouth for a reason. "Even a fool is thought wise if he keeps silent…" (Proverbs 17:28).

**"Men (or women) are like fish. Neither would get into trouble if they kept their mouths shut."** "He who guards his mouth and his tongue keeps himself from calamity" (Proverbs 21:23).

Most of the wisdom shared comes primarily from Proverbs; however, James makes it very clear that the task of controlling your tongue is not easy. In fact, it is impossible unless you tap into the strength only given by God. We find these words in Proverbs 13:3: "He who guards his lips guards his life, but he who speaks rashly will come to ruin." If you need another reminder, Philippians 4:13 confirms that you can do all things through Christ who strengthens you. The manifestation of self-control may seem like it is mind over matter, but it is really a change of heart. The outward appearance of calm collectiveness and the intentionality of your words is the evidence of the newness of life that can only be found in Jesus Christ.

# High Alert: Hurricane Florence

One of the many blessings in my life is the privilege of hosting a "Connect Group" weekly in my home. Our Connect Group is a small group of believers that discuss and study the Word, pray, share concerns, and offer comfort to those in need. One of the persons in our group, Vera, received a profound message that she shared, and with her permission, I am sharing it with you.

During her daily devotional and prayer time, while praying for a close friend who lives near Myrtle Beach, and has decided not to evacuate despite the warnings about Hurricane Florence, Vera journalized the following:

> I cause the rains to fall to the earth.
> I cause the oceans to roar.
> I cause the winds to rage.
> I am in control of all things.
> From gentle rains to the fiercest storm, I am in the midst of it all.

> I would rather you experience my gentleness, but sometimes it is necessary for me to raise my voice. It is then that I am calling all people, groups of people, from every background, to recognize me as their God.

> As the storm rages, my voice raises loud calling people to me. In fear they will come, but only in fear. I would rather be calm and gentle, but a stubborn, rebellious people do not respond to me until I rise up and raise my hand, and destruction comes.

> When this happens, it is a sign of even the calling away, of rapture of the church.

After this storm, you will see one will be taken. Another will be left. Oh, that people would look to me before destruction, but they are sign seekers. Therefore, I will display my anger in hopes for them to call out to me in the time of trouble. The good and the bad will suffer the same fate. Some will come home to me and be safe in my house. Others will go out into eternal darkness. Still others will remain on earth and have the chance to choose me or not.

Destruction and devastation will have its purpose. Many will not understand and say, why God would allow this. I have an eternal purpose in mind, and if my people would turn from their wicked ways and seek my face, none of this would be necessary. You can listen to my small still voice and experience my love and joy, or you can listen to my rage and be in fear and chaos. Both are for the same eternal purpose—that you would enter my presence and know—I am God!

This sharing reminded me of two scriptures: "Those who know your name will trust in you, for you, LORD, have never forsaken those who seek you" (Psalms 9:10). And "As for God, his way is perfect;… He is a shield for all who take refuge in him" (Psalms 18–30).

# Holiday Reflections

What are your expectations for holidays? Do you look forward to spending time with family and friends, or do you like to just "chill" and relax? What has changed, over the years, about the way you spend your holidays?

The recent Memorial Day holiday was a time for reflections of the past, and an excellent opportunity to share pleasant memories of "how things used to be," and what the future may hold. Memories seem to help keep family traditions alive and family ties strong. Overall, how holidays are spent is just another confirmation of Ecclesiastes 3—a time for everything.

A few decades ago, holidays were a perfect time for large family gatherings. In our family, all my siblings (there were seven of us), their mates, and all the children would gather in one place. Many side dishes were prepared the day before, the grills were made ready, volleyball nets were set up, horseshoes were put out, kick balls made available, and the swing sets were cleaned off and made ready for the little ones. In addition to the food tables, there were tables for card games and Scrabble—my favorite! Music played in the background and the atmosphere was filled with laughter and "good conversation." This was the time to "catch up" on what everyone was doing, discuss any concerns, plans, and share answered prayers. Everyone eagerly looked forward to fun games of volleyball, horseshoes, and sometimes softball—depending on whose home we were at and the available space. Then as the day advanced and energy levels dwindled, games like Scattegories and charades entertained the group. There were no cell phones, no Words with Friends, no texting—

thank God! It was just a time for enjoying those that were there and being thankful that we were together one more time.

Time has brought about many changes. Now we are two—instead of seven. Some of the children have even passed on and several are too far away to attend all the holiday gatherings. There are not enough of us still able to play volleyball and we miss those who have gone on; However, we still gather, pray, eat—lots of food, play games, share, and celebrate. The memories we share are lasting and binding treasures, and the many blessings are so apparent.

I am recalling Memorial Day of 2014, family traveled from, California, Michigan, New Jersey, Pennsylvania, and Virginia and joined with our "adopted West Virginia family" as we celebrated just being together. There were no volleyball nets, horseshoes, or kickball. Nevertheless, there was "good conversation," board games, cards, and much sharing, plenty of good food, music, and lots of love!

Things do not stay the same. Just remain flexible and make the best of this life by accepting and adapting to the changes! It works! Read Ecclesiastes 3:1–8.

The cliché "Laugh heartily, love deeply, and pray daily" makes a lot of sense—especially when applied to family. Planning for and expecting to continue with family traditions, gives hope, and a reason to keep on living and loving! There is a time and place for everything! "And we know that in all things God works for the good of those who love Him…" (Romans 8:28).

# How Sound Are Your Investments?

*A*re you spending most of your time monitoring the stock index and trading stock?

Do you worry about the Dow Jones daily market value? Do you have heart palpitations every time the Dow Jones index drops?

Have you arranged your assets in such a manner that you have a diversified portfolio?

Is your focus on an IRA or annuities?

Here is a tip. I hear that there is a stock, USA, which is only $10 a share and includes Apple, Amazon, and a few other major components. They also say the dividends are very good. Are monetary dividends driving what and where you make investments?

It is a wonderful thing to plan and to have financial security, but should that be your priority?

Often, we forget or pay no attention to God's plan for our investing.

The cliché, children are our future, is reality!

The dictionary defines investment as "property, or another possession acquired for future income or benefit." The Bible tells us, "Sons are a heritage from the Lord; Children are a reward from Him" (Psalms 127:3). Does this not give you a clue that this is where you should be investing?

At any given time, there is news about child abuse, neglect, or abandonment. There are also devastating reports about child murderers. There are also reports about all types of child addictions. Would these statistics be less if we gave more attention to investing in our children?

We must be more concerned about investing in our children. Proverbs 6:22, tells us, "Train a child in the way he should go, and when he is old, he will not turn from it."

Teach them…when you are at home. Teach them when you walk along the road. Teach them when you lie down and when you get up.

Take them to Sunday school and church. Read Bible stories to them. Explain the truths of the Bible. Have them learn and memorize scriptures.

Be a Godly example for them. Do your best to keep open communications and a healthy relationship and always show love. Remember, you are the parent, but you can also be a friend.

Be humble and put pride aside if you see that you or they need help in maneuvering through any obstacles or storms, seek help. Know that prayer changes things!

Consider your investments and remember first things first! God has loaned us these precious treasures to bless us. Investing in our children and teaching them is an awesome responsibility and privilege. In Luke 17:2, we find these words, "It would be better for him if a millstone was hung around his neck, and he was thrown into the sea, than he should cause a little one to stumble."

Things happen in life that we cannot control, and we must not punish ourselves for them.

However, know that the dividends for investing in children are unbelievable. The stock market cannot compete with the joy and peace of this sound investment.

# I Am a Masterpiece

*H*as anyone ever said to you, "You are a work of art"? If so, it depends on who said it and why as to how you received those words. It may or may not have been meant as a compliment! Either way, a good response would be, "I know. I am a masterpiece." Each one of us is a unique work of art.

If each one of us would claim this truth, we would realize and know what God wants us to do with our time and our lives. We would strive for purposeful living and recognize that we need to live, love, and serve in this moment. Yesterday is gone, cannot be relived, and tomorrow is not promised. What we have is now!

Remember who you are, and even more important—whose you are. Do not let anyone or anything steal your identity. If you are struggling with temptations and battling demons, remember the price that was paid for you—John 3:16.

When stress mounts up in your life, when pain wracks your body, when grief breaks your heart, or when disappointment shatters your spirit, rest assured that all is well because of whose you are. "For we are God's workmanship, created in Christ Jesus to do good works, which God prepared in advance for us to do" (Ephesians 2:10). You are a masterpiece!

You are not what people may say you are. Do not let yourself be recycled into waste or trash. **You are what God says you are**. Search for, and do not stop searching until you find your true purpose—your passion for living—and be the masterpiece He designed you to be. "But you are a chosen people, a royal priesthood..." (1 Peter 2:9).

Strive for purposeful living, have a vision, and remain unique. Know that your identity rests in God.

As the old cliché says, God do not make no junk!

Believe in yourself. Tell yourself as often as necessary, I am strong; I am special; I can do anything; I am a masterpiece!

# I Can Only Imagine

*W*here does the time go? Recently during a discussion, we reminisced about certain dates in history that were memorable concerning time and/or dates. We were remembering all the concern in 1999 about the widespread predictions of a Y2K computer bug. This bug was predicted to strike on December 31, 1999, and cause technological malfunctions leading to major catastrophes worldwide. It was thought that society would cease to function, and business and industry would come to a standstill. Those professions centered on information systems were more than nervous! People were on stand-by alert to try to rectify hazardous issues and data storage by alternate means was a priority. What a pleasant surprise it was when the New Year's Eve ball dropped, the clock struck midnight, and then 12:01 and there was no major catastrophe with the information systems. I can only imagine what life would have been like if the predicted had happened!

Another prediction was the Rapture of the Christian Church to take place in 1988. I can only imagine!

There have been many predictions and scares that fortunately did not take place. It leaves one to wonder what if these things did happen. One can only imagine.

I can only imagine how different life would be if I had made different decisions in my earlier years and initiated different disciplines into my lifestyle. Experience has taught me that wise choices and maintaining disciplines make a world of difference.

Each morning we wake up is an opportunity to make a new start. What could be a better time to ask God to take your hand as you begin a new day? It is never too late for a new beginning.

Resolutions are not what I am promoting, but try adding a new, positive discipline to your life and maintaining it. Think of it as picking up a new, good habit. Once that habit has roots, pick up another. It may take you a year, or it may only take a few months. Set your own goals. Soon you will find that the new things have replaced the old and there will not be any room for negative things. Vincent van Gogh once said, "Great things are done by a series of small things brought together." So perhaps you might start by thinking about getting in better physical shape. Initial plans might be to walk for a half hour three to four times a week. Then you might add some daily exercises. On the other hand, you might consider becoming a better student of God's Word. You can take on this journey, daily devotions, joining a Bible study group, or increasing your prayer time, etc. So many different avenues.

Remember, while we cannot undo the past, we can start a new thing that could dramatically improve our future. Take the first step and Jesus, the author and finisher of your faith will help you complete what He has called you to begin.

I can only imagine how different, how much better, life will be if I add one new discipline periodically. "Therefore, if anyone is in Christ, the new creation has come: The old has gone, the new is here!" (2 Cor. 5:17). Oh, happy day!

# In the Blink of an Eye

What is a nanosecond? What is PDQ? How long would it take one's life to be forever changed? Consider the things that could possibly happen in the blink of an eye that might forever change the course of your life.

Let fleeting thoughts take you to an unexpected, unwanted phone call in the middle of the night relaying bad news. The immediate impact may be shock, unbelief, and pain, but that call could also change the future course of your life.

In the blink of an eye, a massive heart attack could take one's life. Once again affecting and changing the lives of loved ones.

A stroke can instantaneously interrupt life, change family dynamics, and present detours.

Think about how many are impacted by a lethal drug overdose. In the blink of an eye, life changes forever, for so many.

An automobile accident may not just be inconvenient and frustrating, it too could be deadly, costly, and life-changing. If the accident is caused by someone texting, making a phone call or some other negligent act, the guilt could be devastating!

On the other side of the coin, that phone call could be an offer for a new job and an opportunity to pursue a dream.

In the blink of an eye, you could meet and fall in love with someone you could not live without versus someone you could just live with! There is a BIG difference!

Then there is the lottery! In the blink of an eye, you could be a millionaire! Would this be life-changing?

All these things are rather big items, but how about something as simple as a BM (bile movement) for a baby suffering from colic—relief in the blink of an eye!

Moral: We may not be provided that extra time or opportunity to send up a prayer, so know and believe the scriptures that tell us to "pray without ceasing," and to "be ye also ready." Live and enjoy each day to the fullest, knowing that, Life is Fragile and must be handled with Prayer, because anything can and often does happen, in the blink of an eye.

"Listen, I tell you a mystery: We will not all sleep, but we will all be changed—in a flash, in the twinkling of an eye, at the last trumpet. For the trumpet will sound, the dead will be raised imperishable, and we will be changed" (1 Corinthians 15:51–52).

# Is It Time for a Makeover?

*We* often see contests offering the prize of a complete make-over to the winning contestant. It may be a competition for the most outstanding mother, wife, or husband. Once a winner is chosen, the makeover team takes command. They provide haircuts, hair coloring, and styling. The makeup artists complete the look with enhancements to facial makeup. It might be mascara, eyelashes, cheek coloring, etc. New, stylish attire is also provided. With all the changes in place, the prizewinner is presented to their audience. Everyone is usually very pleased with the outcome and there are plenty of happy amazed faces. How long will this change last? Will they be able to maintain this new look? Can they afford to maintain the new look?

There are also homes that undergo the makeover process. The designers and construction crews come in, redo, and refurnish a home in a short period. They paint, add windows, change lighting, and redo flooring. The new space is almost unrecognizable when they finish the job. Often with these makeover homes, the changes occur both on the inside and on the outside of the home. These changes are more permanent. They often involve structural changes that could be equated to putting a strong foundation in place.

What about you? Are you in need of a makeover? It is not often that we ordinary folk get to appear on the Oprah show or Today show for a makeover; but we do not need that kind of publicity. 2 Corinthians 5:17 tells us, "If anyone is in Christ, he is a new creation; the old has gone, the new has come."

Walk with me to Romans 10:9–13, "Confess with your mouth, 'Jesus is Lord,' and believe in your heart that God raised him from the dead, you will be saved. For it is with your heart that you believe and are justified, and it is with your mouth that you confess and are saved…" You do not need to enter a competition or write any story. This is the only makeover team or construction crew needed. This change will make you magnificent inside and out. It will not just be a surface change. It is one you can afford and maintain. You can now truthfully claim what you are and whose you are. Leave all negative comments, remarks, and baggage where they started. Move on! Do not dwell on aches and pain. Concentrate only on happy things and hope. "For in my inner being I delight in God's law" (Romans 7:22).

So whether this is a new beginning, or you are looking for some self-improvement, it is always a good time to consider a makeover!

# It's a Personal Thing

*H*aving on-going projects to work on during idle time, TV time, nighttime relaxation before going to sleep, or when traveling, helps me feel like I am taking full advantage of the gift of time that I have been given. In the closet, there are varieties of fully equipped tote bags. One tote bag is complete with knitting needles, markers, yarn, and instructions. Another tote has a crochet hook, yarn, measuring tape, and crochet directions or pattern. In addition, there are a couple of different totes with varying levels of cross-stitch projects. Which project comes out of the closet depends on the length of travel time and whether it is a car trip, bus trip, and who happens to be my traveling partner.

Pondering through the cross-stitch corner in preparation for an up-coming trip, I came across a notepad that contained a variety sayings and clichés waiting to be stitched on bookmarks, greeting cards, hand towels, quilts, or whatever! These quotes came from various sources and places and unfortunately, I do not know whom to designate as the originator. Sharing these "nuggets" might serve as "food for thought" and cause you to smile, inspire you to change something in your life, motivate you to do something different or just bring back a memory. Give them some thought!

A good neighbor is a welcome blessing.

When I count my blessings, I think of you.

Faithful, thankful, blessed.

A friend is a family member we have been able to choose.

Take time to pray.

Home is where the heart is

I believe in angels.

Friends make life bloom.

Plant kindness. Gather love.

Prayers are the stairs to God.

No act of kindness, no matter how small is ever wasted.

I am wealthy in my friends.

Give yourself permission to be young again.

Friendship grows with tender loving care.

"Love is my decision to make your problems my concern" (Schuller).

"Jesus Christ, the same yesterday, and today and forever" (Hebrews 13:8).

Where there is great love, there are always miracles.

Your presence is a present to the world.

Life's treasures are people together.

It is a great thing to be faithful in little things.

If we defend our habits, we have no intention of changing them...

Success requires backbones, not wishbones.

Instead of a plate, reach for your mate.

The road to hell is paved with "good intentions."

All of us can be compared to nuts—peanuts, pecans, walnuts, hickory nuts. All get broken to get the goodies!

What you think, feel, or do is a personal thing!

"So I saw that there is nothing better for a man than to enjoy his work, because that is his lot. For who can bring him to see what will happen after him?" (Ecclesiastes 3:22).

# It's All about the Name

"'Tis the season to be jolly!" When we hear those words, we are reminded that it is nearing time for a visit from jolly old St. Nicholas, AKA Santa Claus. Children's ears are perked, best behaviors surface, and parents either are in a shopping frenzy, busy placing mail orders, or wrapping and hiding presents. The name Santa Claus causes a metamorphosis among both adults and children. Although often frazzled, Christmas is generally a happy time. And Santa Claus remains a popular well-known name!

There is a woman, not-so-well-known, Jan Alexuk. Jan is affectionately known as the "sticker lady"! Why? Jan decorates envelopes with stickers and sends greeting cards to kids, seniors, military families and many more. It is said that she spends fifteen to twenty minutes, picking just the right stickers to decorate each envelope. Why? Because the recipients enjoy the stickers and feel the love. This is Jan's ministry. Her stickers make people happy!

When we lived in Pittsburgh, my daughter was often embarrassed as we walked through the mall or Giant Eagle to hear, "Hey, there's the 'gas lady.'" It let her know that some unfortunate customer had apparently been working with me to restore gas service that had been terminated for nonpayment. It often was not a pleasant experience for me either. However, hearing the term "gas lady" put us on guard! "Gas lady" was my identity.

Why were you given your name? Do you know what your name means? Does your name fit your personality or your gift? Maybe it is time for you to do a little research on the meaning of your name. Give it some thought.

Being that Jesus is the reason for this season, let's look at that wonderful name, and the peace and comfort we can find in that name and the other names of God.

There are many names for God. Each one describes a wonderful aspect of His multifaceted character. Know that these are not the names of multiple gods, but they are all names for our one amazing, awesome God! Some of the names from the Old Testament are as follows:

Jehovah, M Kaddesh, or "the God who sanctifies" (Leviticus 20:7–8)

Jehovah Jireh or "the God who provides" (Genesis 22:9–14)

Jehovah Shalom or "the God of peace" (Judges 6:16–24)

Jehovah Rapha or "Jehovah heals" (Exodus 15:22–26)

Jehovah Nissi or "God our banner" (Exodus 17:8–15)

El-Shaddai or "God Almighty" (Genesis 49:22–26)

Adonai or "Master" or "Lord" (Samuel 7:18–20)

Elohim or "Strength" or "Power" (Genesis 17:7–8)

Some of the more familiar names are the following:

**Almighty** (Revelations 1:8): Meaning Jesus is all-powerful. Nothing is beyond His reach.

**Messiah** (Jesus is Messiah): Appointed by God for His plan and purpose.

**Redeemer**: Jesus is our redemption. Christ's death is the payment for all our sins.

**Savior**: Jesus is our salvation. He is the one who seeks and saves the lost.

**Son of God**: Jesus is the Son of God by nature. Christ is the only "natural" Son of God.

**The Way, the Truth, and the Life**: Jesus is our path to God.

**Bread of Life:** Jesus is our sustenance. He is our spiritual nourishment and the sustenance of the world.

**Bright Morning Star**: Jesus lights our way. We shall not lose our way in His light.

Born in Bethlehem on Christmas Day, **Jesus is the reason to celebrate this season.**

It is all about the name! Happy birthday, Jesus.

Merry Christmas to you all as you joyfully celebrates His birthday!

# It's in the Bag

*I* am a bag lady.

It is okay. I admit it and I accept that title. Bags help keep some organization in my life.

I have an identifiable bag for current crochet projects. This bag contains yarn, crochet hooks, scissors, large-eyed needle to weave in threads and any necessary instructions.

The counted cross-stitch project is also in a bag. This bag has the Aida cloth, embroidery hoops, floss, needles and folding scissors, and cross-stitch alphabet patterns.

Then there is a bag for recycling grocery/shopping bags—which we recycle and use to line all the small waste cans throughout the house.

I have a tote bag that I use to carry things up and down stairs. This frees up my hands so at least one hand is always on the rails.

Each morning begins with a special bright pink tote that has several pockets. This tote contains my daily devotional books, a Bible, a notepad, highlighter markers, pencils, pen, and Post-it notes. This tote has a home on the corner of the sofa in my bedroom. After taking care of personal hygiene, I make a cup of coffee, snuggle on the sofa, under the window, and start my daily ritual of prayer and reading the variety of devotionals in my tote. As I read, I often get thoughts that make me pause to journal. This journaling often leads to the articles that I write, and you read.

Making tote bags is a hobby I enjoy. Most of these bags are used as gift bags.

All of the bags mentioned so far are tangible made of some type of fabric. Now I will share a bag of clichés or quotes that I have recorded in a notebook. Sort through them and store the useful ones in your personal memory bag. And do not be surprised if you see them on a bookmark or card that I have made. Who knows, you might consider becoming a bag person too.

- Begin to weave and God will give the thread.
- Good character, like good soup, is made at home.
- Words must be weighed, not counted.
- Rejoice in the Lord always (Phil. 4:4).
- Never be afraid to try, remember, amateurs built the ark. Professionals built the *Titanic* (Unknown).
- Great minds have purposes, others have wishes (Washington Irving).
- God gives us the nuts, but He does not crack them.
- Friends who take time to care are really angels unaware.
- Any jackass can kick down a barn, but it takes a good carpenter to build one.
- Dollars and sense should go together.
- Friends come and go, but enemies accumulate.
- Faith makes things possible…not always easy.
- Shoot for the moon. Even if you miss, you will land among the stars.
- God is faithful—all the time.

Finally, this thought should always be in memory bag. God loves you today—every single moment, in every possible way, through every circumstance, with all His heart.

# January Celebrations

*D*uring the month of January, excitement has been in the air. Beginning with all the New Year gala, parades, and festivities, then I was blessed to see another birthday. Next, we had the Martin Luther King Holiday and more celebrations, including time off from school and many had a day off from work. Perhaps the biggest celebration of the month was the presidential inauguration! While there seems to be some controversy over the numbers gathered at, and/or watching this historical event, we all know it happened, so what does it matter about the numbers? One thing for sure, we have been provided with some great entertainment (my opinion) from Saturday Night Live featuring Alec Baldwin to the Jimmy Fallon and Seth Myers shows.

It appears that a vast number of us are upset and perhaps overly concerned about America's future. Healthcare, deportation, and discrimination are only a few of the areas that concern ordinary people. **But it's all in God's hands.** Perhaps this election is what it took Christians to truly begin claiming His promises like "I will never leave you nor forsake you"—and to begin "pray without ceasing." This does not mean that we must be continually prone or on our knees, but to have a prayerful attitude!

The shift we have witnessed in government is what it is. At this point in time, whether we are happy or sad about the outcome of the 2016 election results, there is absolutely nothing we can do to change things. Therefore, if you are among the dissatisfied, what we can do is totally rely of our biblical faith! Claim and adopt the FROG mentality—**f**ully **r**ely **on G**od for the future! Know that…

"**All** things work together for good to them that love God, to them who are called according to *his* purpose" (Romans 8:28).

He is the "same" God, yesterday, today, and tomorrow. That says to me, He is the same God we served and relied on before the inauguration, and He is the same God after the inauguration. Check out Jeremiah 17:7. Keep the faith and be blessed!

# Jewels Are Precious

*M*ost of us are familiar with the old cliché, "Diamonds are a girl's best friend." Are they really? What jewels do you consider precious and why?

Diamonds and jewels are accessories that can and often do complement an outfit. They sparkle and attract attention. Some jewels are very bright, easily noticed, recognized by name, and admired for their value. Some jewels while still very beautiful, their appearance is subtle, clean, and even fragrant.

The *Today Show* did a segment on jewels this week. It pertained to using jewels, inexpensive ones, to add character and beauty to common household items. They suggested taking a plain hand mirror, like the ones often found in bathrooms, and gluing jewels around the frame. The addition of the jewels made a plain item very attractive. These tangible jewels brightened the entire space. It seemed worth the time and effort.

Listening as they described the task and rationale of creating beautiful objects for the home, my thoughts drifted to the jewels that are only found in salvation. Jewels always present for us to adorn are daily Bible study, prayer, love for one another, and discipline. These jewels help us become strong and gives us power to soar like an eagle. As a bonus, strength, hope, peace, and joy are present. Are these not precious jewels? These jewels are not tangible for you to touch or run your hand over, but they are visible through your actions, deeds, and the way you live your life. Perhaps it is time to coin a new cliché about precious jewels! Let us give that some thought.

Isaiah 54:11–12 tells us, "I will make your battlements of rubies, your gates of sparkling jewels, and all your walls of precious stones." Does that not sound better than a sparkling hand mirror?

# Kick Off Summer the Right Way

Summer is a season when comfort is ambiguous. We want it hot, but we seem to need the air conditioner. So we totter between having the air conditioner on high to basking in the sun for a tan. Others prefer fresh air flowing through the house and sunshine beaming through the windows. Whatever your preference, the sun seems to be the center of attraction for many.

The sun brings brightness to the long summer days, is refreshing, and seems to help many have a more positive attitude. Many get their fill of sun and excitement from a cruise or a beach vacation. Others may enjoy camping, hiking, or bicycling.

Working in the sun and taking pride in your yard and/or gardening allows one to be creative, get some exercise and fresh air while providing an esthetic environment for all who pass by. It is amazing how many benefits from one person's energy and care of their outside surroundings.

Whether you are working in the sun, playing in the sun, or just relaxing in the sun, wear that sunbonnet, or cap. Sunscreen is for your protection—use it lavishly. Make sure you stay hydrated and drink plenty of fluids. Be aware of how long you are exposed to the sun. Use common sense and guard your health! The sun gives us vitamin D, makes you feel better, and brings out the melanin in your skin. It makes you feel sun "kissed"—a good feeling. Yet the sunrays can be harmful and can cause serious health issues.

Mind that while you are enjoying the sun and all these outside activities, you must be careful and take precautions from the sun. The sun is not like the spiritual "Son," where there is no need to protect yourself. You can bask in His comfort, goodness, love, and peace and the benefits are mercy and grace. If you let the "Son" shine in, there will be no worry about sunburn or dehydration. Instead, you will find a warm heart and a willingness to put love in action.

"May those who love you be like the sun when it rises in its strength" (Judges 5:31).

Kick off your summer the right way and let the "Son" shine in!

# Know When to Hold and When to Fold

*B*ack in the eighties, one of my favorite artists, Kenny Rogers, recorded a song, "You gotta know when to hold 'em, when to fold 'em, and when to walk away." This song skyrocketed on the billboards and won him much recognition and awards. The theme of the song is about the skill of a successful gambler. It gives pointed advice on how one should act or interact in a poker game. Kenny makes it very clear that if you are gonna play the game, you must learn to play it right.

That same advice is applicable to how we should live our lives. The only difference is that life is not a game.

If you were to get in a hot air balloon, the wind determines your fate. While attempting to guide the balloon, you can only push so hard against the winds. There might be times when a quick decision must be made to land—even if you are off course. In this case, you must know when to push, and when to let go and land. Your safety and possibly your life depend on knowing when to fold.

When tempted to do things that could potentially harm you, saying, "Not today, Satan," may not be enough. Know that you must be willing to turn and run—not walk—away from the evil. "Be self-controlled and alert. Your enemy the devil prowls around like a roaring lion, looking for someone to devour. Resist him, standing firm in the faith…" (1 Peter 5:8–9). Know when to fold and get away!

In this song, the gambler knows the way, shows the way, and goes the way.

This is an example of how we, as Believers, must live our lives. We know the way. We must be willing to show others the way to salvation. In addition, we must stand firm in our faith, and when tempted, know who to turn and run to, and do it.

The song implies that when gambling, knowing when to hold, when to fold, and when to walk away leads to success. God does not command us to be successful. He commands us to be faithful and to trust in His Word. So knowing when to hold, when to fold, and when to walk away does have application to our Christian walk. Kenny Rogers delivered a powerful message in the eighties that still resonates today.

# Learning to Love

*L*ast week one of the devotionals that I read had a message about the Zax Nature. The Zax is a Dr. Seuss character. This message caused me to retrieve and reread Dr. Suess's book, *Sneetches and Other Stories*. This book was written in 1961 to teach children about discrimination. The book consists of four short stories with themes of tolerance, diversity, and compromise.

The first story, Star-Belly Sneetches, tells of the Sneetches on the beach. Some of the Sneetches had stars on their belly and were called Star-Belly Sneetches. The others that inhabited the beach were plain. They were referred to as Plain-Belly Sneetches. The Star-Belly Sneetches believed themselves superior and better than Plain-Belly Sneetches and all their actions promoted this belief of entitlement and privilege. These ideas were taught to their children and this hateful tradition was passed on through the years. ("Train a child in the way he should go, and when he is old, he will not turn from it" [Proverbs 22:6]). "If anyone teaches false doctrines and does not agree to the sound instruction of our Lord Jesus Christ and to godly teaching, he is conceited and understands nothing" (1 Timothy 6:3–4).

One day, Sylvester McMonkey McBean (a shyster) came to town with his magnificent invention. He had a contraption that would put stars on the Plain-Belly Sneetches, for a small fee. The contraption worked. Now all the Sneetches looked the same. The original Star-Belly Sneetches were quite dissatisfied and unhappy. McBean then offered to remove their stars, for a slightly higher fee. They went through the change. Had their stars removed, but they still had this superiority complex. A vicious cycle of adding stars and removing stars continued until McBean had taken all their money. It was at this point that they realized that they were all Sneetches—stars or no stars—there were similarities that connected them. "Those who seemed to be important-whatever they were makes no difference to me; God does not judge by external appearances..." (Galatians 2:6).

What a good lesson on antiracism and equality!

The second story is the Zax. There was a North-Going Zax and a South-Going Zax, travelling in the prairie of Prax. Although they had different destinations, they were on the same path. They reached a point where they met, face to face on the path, and neither was willing to go east or west to let the other pass. They argued, and stood firm, vowing not to budge even if the whole world had to stand still. They were stubborn, committed to the idea that they were right. The world did not standstill for them. The world grew and built highways and buildings all around them. They were left stuck where they stood. Is that not self-destruction?

They were unwilling to compromise and be tolerant of each other's needs. In Philippians 4:2 Paul says, "I plead with Euodia and Syntyche to agree with each other in the Lord." Whatever conflict they were having, Paul calls them out, knowing that God lovingly chooses to soften stubborn hearts. "Make my joy complete by being like-minded..." (Philippians 2:2). Apparently this did not happen for the Zaxes.

The next story, "Too Many Daves," is about not making good choices. Mrs. McCave had twenty-three children—all boys, and she named them all Dave. Can you imagine the chaos when she called for Dave? She wished she had made a better decision, but it was too late. "Do not exasperate your children, instead bring them up in the training and instruction of the Lord" (Ephesians 6:4).

The last story in the book is "What was I scared of?" This cute story is about confronting and facing your fears. The Sneetch kept encountering a pair of empty green pants. This was a new sight for him, so he not only avoided the empty green pants, but he also ran from them. In an unintended encounter with the empty green pants, he realized there was nothing to fear. The empty green pants just looked different. "I sought the Lord, and He answered me; He delivered me from all my fears" (Psalms 34:4).

From discrimination, arguments, disagreements, poor decisions, and most of all our fears and misunderstandings… God is there to guide us. He has given us instruction and comfort when confronted with any litany of issues that we may face. I am reminded of one of my favorite scriptures, "Trust in the Lord with all thine heart, and lean not to thine own understanding" (Proverbs 3:5–6).

We must learn to accept people for who they are. Look for similarities, not differences. After all the scriptures tell us, "Love each other" (John 15:17).

# Lest We Forget

*J*uly 4—Independence Day, Freedom Day—a time for celebration and thankfulness. As usual, this holiday and this week has been all about celebrating and remembering what our country is supposed to stand for. There are parades, special media broadcasts, fireworks, flying flags and in the midst—senseless killings, random acts of violence, outbursts of blatant prejudice and frightening misuse of opiates and other lethal drugs. Where have we come from? Where are we going? Many look to the Statue of Liberty as a symbol of our freedom. Is it? Lest we forget…

Most of us know about and are familiar with the word amnesia—the partial or total loss of memory. This condition can be caused by shock, some psychological disturbance, brain injury, or illness. Recently I became aware of the term—spiritual amnesia. In two different devotionals, this term appeared and resonated with me. The one devotional dealt with pride, and how so many of us try to define ourselves by our personal accomplishments. We associate our worth by what we've done, instead of in whom we belong. We want our achievements, our victories, our trophies, our wins, our degrees, our titles to define us instead of acknowledging God as the source of all good things. Our story is, "Look at me and what I have done!"

How many of us want to take all the credit for the liberties we exercise and enjoy, and the accomplishments achieved, and be known as someone who "has it all together"? Intoxicating pride intercedes and the inevitable hangover is our way of life. This is when we lose our destined identity and begin suffering from spiritual amnesia. We forget who brought us to where we are!

If we want to truly be free, we must grow humble, and not only fight pride, but defeat pride. The same is true with bondage and addictions. The goal is not to just fight, but to overcome. Prejudice is another struggle that we must fight and defeat. Perhaps we could cure our spiritual amnesia by indulging in a simple daily prayer like "Today help me overcome any struggle by remembering the source of my freedom."

"You have been set free from sin and have become slaves to righteousness" (Romans 6:18).

"So if the Son sets you free, you will be free indeed" (John 8:36).

"It is for freedom that Christ has set us free. Stand firm, then, and do not let yourselves be burdened again by a yoke of slavery" (Galatians 5:1–2).

What does God need to change in you for you to be free, and for you to allow others their freedom?

Lest we forget, the Cross is the only true Statue of Liberty!

# Let's Do a Makeover

*T*his is the season when there seems to be a strong focus on weight and weight loss. It is hot and we wear less clothing. There are no heavy winter coats or bulky sweaters to cover the bulges, and many are frantically indulging in quick guaranteed weight loss programs, fitness programs, body sculpting, and even liposuction. We want a better-looking body for the shorts and swimsuits. We realize that all the indulgences and lack of activity over the winter months suddenly are very noticeable. Notably WeightWatchers gets a spike in memberships this time of the year! We are all looking for a makeover!

Every so often different TV programs or celebrities offer viewers an opportunity for a makeover. Most often, it is a mother, but sometimes it is a dad or husband that is brought in for this awesome task.

The teams of make-up artists usually do a fantastic job, trimming or cutting and coloring hair, applying make-up, donning good under garments, and supplying an attractive, becoming outfit. The benefactor of this once in a lifetime service, often appears ten to twenty years younger, vibrant, lean, and happy.

The new outside appearance is usually marketed with a tag, "easy to maintain," and everyone seemingly goes away pleased.

Several scriptures also deal with a makeover:

> "Behold, the former things have come to pass, and new things I now declare…" (Isaiah 42:9)

"Therefore if anyone is in Christ, he is a new creation. The old has passed away; behold the new has come." (2 Corinthians 5:17)

"Behold, I am making everything new..." (Revelation 21:5)

Only God can do on the inside what the makeup artists do on the outside. The scars on our hearts and the imprints on our minds can only be removed and transformed into masterpieces of beauty through His grace and mercy. When this happens not only will we be blessed, but also all those around us will be blessed as they witness the change and the beauty that comes from within. With this makeover, not only will you look different, your walk and your talk will be different.

Time for a makeover that is easy to maintain? Just as Jesus tells his disciples in John 14, "Do not let your hearts be troubled. Trust in God; trust also in me." Be blessed!

# Little and Small Things Really Matter

*S*ome say, "It's the little things in life that count." I would agree that this is true, especially when it comes to deeds, gestures, and freely given compliments and/or acts of love. On the other hand, think on these things...

Think about a little pimple that suddenly appears on your cheek just about the time of an important engagement or social affair. Does that little thing stress you out? It definitely gets your attention.

If you have ever had a corn or bunion on your toe, you will know the pain or discomfort that little thing can cause.

Those folks that have experienced a hangnail, will attest to that uncomfortable feeling.

An in-grown hair can also cause some pain, misery and maybe even a scar depending on the location.

If an eyelash or speck of dust gets in your eye, you will notice tears, burning, itching, and much discomfort, until it is removed.

Small particles of food stuck between your teeth may not be uncomfortable but can certainly cause bad breath. That is why, in addition to brushing your teeth and rinsing with mouthwash, flossing is a must! Breath mints will not cut it. When the mint is gone, the odor will still be there. Trust me!

Have you ever had a pebble or grains of sand in your shoe? You cannot rest until it is removed. Such a small thing, but a huge annoyance!

Little words like *and* and *but* often serve as a warning of a consequence or something to watch out for. Be careful of how and when you use these words.

A minute, such a small amount of time, can be critical in a medical crisis such as a stroke. Misusing a few seconds of time, like texting while driving, can be more damaging and deadly that anyone would even dare imagine. A very small portion of time, but how costly might it be.

On the positive side, a warm smile could brighten someone's day. A pat on the back might be just the encouragement someone needs to keep on living! A kind word could bring peace and comfort to a lonely soul. A gentle touch might be just the spark needed to allow someone to see that there are brighter days ahead and that they are not alone. Think about the little things that we often take for granted. These things are there to remind us of the God's grace, mercy, and splendor. Sunsets, beautiful night skies, laughter, flowers, warm breezes, glimpses of fond memories, and acts of kindness…all of these things may seem small or unnoticeable, but when we notice and are thankful for the little things we begin to shine, and the *Son* shines through us. My suggestion is that we not only notice and give thanks, but we fully engage in the supposedly small offerings. Do little things to brighten others' day. Your thoughtfulness could be life-changing.

"For whoever keeps the whole law and yet stumbles at just one point is guilty of breaking all of it" (James 2:10).

# Little Words Matter

*F*our-letter words are often a topic of conversation. As you know, some of these words are vulgar and offensive by nature and others are perceived vulgar by choice. An example of choice would be work, play, stop, etc....

What are your thoughts about two-letter words? Personally, I like them and use them as often as I can.

After finally coercing some friends to play a game of Scrabble, and then being ribbed about my vocabulary, my thoughts began to focus on words, the meaning of words, and the perception of words. Being an avid Scrabble player, I have learned that other than using seven-letter words to earn those extra fifty points, two-letter words, strategically placed are often the strongest plays. Many opponents get frustrated when you spell two-letter words—especially those that are unfamiliar to them. Some complain that you should be able to make a sentence using the word for it to be acceptable. They are the whiners! However, strategically playing *xi*, *xu*, *qi*, *za*, or *fe* has often put me in the winner's seat. So be it!

Two-letter words are not only important in Scrabble and Words with Friends, but they can also be critical in conveying thoughts and reaching understandings. The word if, for example, often implies, maybe, or it could just mean conditionally. Wanting to get a better feel on what others thought about two-letter words, I decided to do a random survey of favorite two-letter words. The question was, what is your favorite two-letter word and why. These are some of the responses:

> ***No***: Because it was recently made public that many people said no, but still became victims. No matters.
>
> ***No***: One of the first words taught to babies and toddlers—more for protection than for reprimand.
>
> ***No***: Took years for me to feel comfortable enough to be able to say no. Now I can handle it.
>
> ***We***: includes others.
>
> ***Go***: Like to get up and go.
>
> ***Is***: It is what it is.
>
> ***We***: It is not just about me.
>
> ***Me***: It is all about me.
>
> ***Or***: It gives me a choice.
>
> ***Si***: It's a fragrance I have been wearing all summer.
>
> ***If/or***: Think about if I had done this or if I had not done this…
>
> ***Ya***: What my kids said instead of yes and it just brings back fond memories.
>
> ***By***: Good gaming two-letter word. As you can see, "no" was the most popular. No one chose to, it, okay, up, or any of the favored high-point Scrabble words like qi, xi, pi, or jo.

After much thought, I want to share my favorite two-letter word. It is **so**. Why? "God *so* loved the world that he gave his one and only son, that whoever believes in him shall not perish but have eternal life" (John 3:16).

According to David Jeremiah, so is the biggest little word in the Bible. So may not give you those big scores in Scrabble, but it paves the way for grace and mercy! So be it!

# Love the Word

Words are fascinating. Receiving a Scrabble Set for Christmas when I was about eight years old (a very long time ago) gave me a deep appreciation for words and thereby started this fascination. Studying for "spelling bees" was my "thing." Memorizing the periodic table in Chemistry and the root words in Latin class kept me a step ahead of my older siblings. One example of education giving one an advantage!

Many never think about the power of words. Being one of the most common means of communication, whether they are big words, little words or unusual words, words always convey a feeling or thought!

Words can build up or tear down. Words like "I love you," "You are beautiful," and "You are a good boy" do a lot to build self-esteem and self-confidence. On the other hand, "I hate you," "You're fat," "You're stupid," "You're so sloppy" may just have the opposite effect.

A baby's much-anticipated first words are exciting. Everyone makes over baby and soon more words follow. That is a good thing.

You can often tell the educational level of a person by their use of words, or lack thereof. For instance, when someone constantly uses profane words, to me, it is an indication that they have little respect for others and very little self-respect. Words can paint a picture.

Twisting of words or taking them out of context can have devastating consequences. Think about how the "serpent" twisted what God said to Adam and Eve about the fruit in the Garden of Eden. Compare that to how the manipulative words of a charismatic leader can easily persuade folks that everyone is going to heaven no matter what their religion is. Words have power!

IF you have a habit of using some of those offensive four-letter words, try substituting them with *love, pray, work, read*, or *save*. Then try this little tactic: get a large rubber band and put it on your wrist. Every time you utter a "bad" word or think a negative thought, snap the rubber band. If you do that faithfully, I am willing to bet that you will soon drop that habit!

This love/fascination with words often leads me to make acronyms. So here goes, WORDS:

W for *wisdom*: Gain wisdom in all that you do.

O for *order*: Do things decent and in order.

R for *respect*: Learn to respect yourself and show respect for others.

D for *devoted*: Be devoted to studying His Word and knowing what it says.

S for *saved*: Get saved—self-explanatory!

The love of words opened the door for love of The Word!

Reading and studying The Word will help you hear "alarm bells" about right and wrong decisions, and Satan's ploys to deceive you. Use the Word to fight those enemies and win any battle. I have learned and experienced that The Word guides us. The Word give us Faith. The Word encourages us. The Word equips us.

Let the Word "be a lamp unto your feet, and a light unto your path."

Then you can honestly and sincerely say, "May the words of my mouth and the meditation of me heart be pleasing in your sight..." (Psalms 19:14).

# Menial

There is no such thing as a menial job. How many times have you heard someone say, "I am just a _____," referring to their employment or personal status? It seems that many folks just do not realize their value.

Is it because in our society we have a strong silent caste system, treating people different because of their job title or position? Are we causing people to feel inferior because of the work they do? Are you guilty of shunning someone because of the type of work they perform? Why? We all have different talents and abilities, and it takes them working together to get the job done.

Every job has expectations and if those expectations are clearly communicated, you can be on your way to success. Knowing what needs to be done gives you the opportunity to meet or perhaps even exceed expectations. Your job, whatever it is, is important for things to run smoothly.

Would not it be GREAT if we could get people to understand that they are valuable, and necessary, for the service they perform? If you are an Assistant whatever—think about the load you are carrying for whomever you are assisting. If you are a substitute teacher, could the schools function as efficiently without you?

If you are one of those persons that refer to yourself as "just a _____," or if you know someone that does that, go to Romans 10:12 for starters, and imbed that verse in your heart and mind. However, if you are guilty of looking down on someone because of their position or status, know that you most likely are enjoying the benefits of their labor. Instead of feeling superior, be appreciative and grateful for the services they provide.

Think about an automobile. How would it go without gas? How far could it go without tires? Would it be able to run without a battery? It takes many parts for that Cadillac to even move. Some of the parts are more expensive than others, but each part has a function, and all are needed for a smooth comfortable ride. Likewise, it takes all of us and our talents to make the world go round.

Know that each one of us is unique and put here for a purpose. Find that purpose and "be steadfast, immoveable, always abounding in the work of the Lord, knowing that in the Lord your labor is not in vain."

# What Do You See?

*P*eople look into mirrors to see how they look. They look into the Psalms to find out who they are.

A mirror is an excellent way to learn about our appearance. The Psalms are the biblical way to discover ourselves.

With a mirror, we detect a new wrinkle here, an old wart there and perhaps some new gray hairs. We use a mirror when shaving or applying make-up to improve, if we can, the face we present to the world.

Take a minute and think about the different types of mirrors. At the amusement parks, we find mirrors that give comical body illusions—elongating the body, smashing the body, making you look fat or twisted. Then there are the magnifying mirrors enlarging your features sometimes as much as five times and revealing every pore and hair on your face. These contortions are most often not gratifying, but they do provide an image. However, the images we see in these mirrors are not honest and true reflections.

With the Psalms we bring into awareness an ancient sorrow, release a latent joy as we present ourselves before God as honestly and thoroughly as we are able.

A mirror shows us the shape of our nose and the curve of our chin, things we otherwise know only through the report of others. The Psalms show us the shape of our souls and the curve of our sins, realities deep within us, hidden and obscured, for which we need focus and names. Could it be anger, shame, or guilt that we have tried to hide?

The poetry of the Psalms tell us what our eyes, blurred with too much gawking, and our ears, dulled with too much chatter and loud music, miss around and within us.

While a mirror helps us to cover flaws, change the shape of our eyebrows, the Psalms requires that we deal with our actual humanity. The life-settings of the Psalms are not geographical or cultural but INTERIOR. Calvin called the Psalms "an anatomy of all the parts of the soul." Everything that anyone can feel or experience in relation to God is found in the Psalms. You will find the Psalms the best place to explore and dissect all the parts of your life and then to say who you are and what is in you—guilt, anger, salvation, praise…

Check out your physical image in the mirror, but if you want to check out the real you, and get a true and honest image, study the Psalms.

# MOPS, CEOS, and Others...

*H*ave you ever attended a meeting, or been in conversation with someone and had no clue what they were talking about? Too often the use of acronyms and abbreviations leave non-professionals at a disadvantage. Throwing terms around without explaining can cause a lot of frustration and feelings of inadequacy.

It seems that different professions, organizations, and businesses all have their own lingo. Moreover, if you have not had a "short course" in that jargon, you might lag behind in the conversation.

For instance, many people are not familiar with MOPS. If someone stopped you on the street and began a conversation about MOPS, what would be your first thoughts? You might think they were trying to sell you a cleaning apparatus.

MOPS, however, is a faith-based organization for Mothers of Preschoolers. These moms meet on a regular basis, fellowship, share ideas, and collaborate on the joys, frustrations, and difficulties of parenting. It is a wonderful opportunity for these young women to get together, have someone to confide in and share what is happening in their lives. It is refreshing to know that they are not alone and to be reminded just how special it is to be a mother.

CEOS (Community Educational Outreach Service) are groups/clubs affiliated with the land grants colleges in each state. In West Virginia, WVU Extension Service supports the CEOS. The mission of the West Virginia Community Educational Outreach Service (WVCEOS) is to strengthen individuals and families through Continuing Education, Community Service, and Leadership Development. There are several clubs in each county, with members doing all kinds of volunteer work.

The point is this: when engaging someone in a conversation, doing a presentation or just in general conversation, be clear about initials, acronyms, or language that might just be common a particular group.

Almost everyone is familiar with BLT. Bacon, lettuce, and tomato has been around for a long time. While sitting in my daughter's office, a few years ago, I kept hearing the term PD. Believe me, it took a while before I figured out, they were talking about Professional Development. One that I learned from reading Oprah's magazine is DIY—do it yourself. We all can think of times to use that one. In my previous employment, CGIs were common jargon—cannot get in. This was an alert that needed action.

N/A still has several meanings, and it depends on the situation. On an application form, n/a could mean not applicable. On a delivery route it would mean no access. It could also mean not available.

LOL is another confusing one. My concept of LOL is *lots of love*, and I was closing e-mails and text messages to nieces and nephews with LOL, only to be advised that LOL is *laughing out loud*. What a difference a generation makes!

Let us learn to set the stage and keep the playing field level. Explain yourself and your jargon. Be clear.

In addition, be especially clear that when you speak about our Lord and Savior Jesus Christ. Do not become so lax that you refer to Him as JC. Many might think you said JZ! And that would not be cool!

"Write…and make it plain…so that heralds may run with it" (Habakkuk 2:2).

# Nature versus Pills

It seems that as we mature pills invade and sometimes bombard our lives. Tests often reveal that, according to some recommended levels, the cholesterol levels are high, and the so-called cure is a pill! Then a checkup shows that your blood pressure numbers are not where the chart says they should be. The answer—another pill. Soon after that checkup, there is swelling in your ankles and legs and the diagnosis is, you are retaining too much water and you need to take a "water pill." Arthritis pain pushes you toward the medicine cabinet for a "pain pill," and while you are there, you reach for that daily aspirin you take as a precaution against a heart attack, or whatever. Meanwhile all these "helps" are eating away the lining of your stomach and intestines, and you soon develop bleeding ulcers, which you will need another pill to correct those symptoms.

The vicious cycle continues! Could there possibly be another solution rather than constantly swallowing pills and capsules?

A friend shared the following information with me and, although I have not verified the stated research, the information is interesting and worthy of consideration.

The story of the creation tells us that God first separated the salt water from the fresh, made dry land, planted a garden, made animals and fish, and then He made a human. He made and provided what we would need before we were born. Isn't that just like a father?

God left us a great clue as to what foods help what part of our body! God's pharmacy is amazing! Check this out!

A sliced **carrot** looks like the human eye. The pupil, iris, and the radiating lines look just like the human eye...and yes, science now shows carrots greatly enhance blood flow to promote the function of the eyes.

The **tomato** has four chambers and is red. The heart has four chambers and is red. Research shows that tomatoes are loaded with lycopene and are good heart and blood food.

**Grapes** hang in a cluster that has the shape of the heart. Each grape looks like a blood cell and research today shows that grapes are also a profound heart and blood vitalizing food.

A **walnut** looks like a little brain, a left and right hemisphere, upper cerebrums, and lower cerebellums. Even the wrinkles or folds on the nut are very similar to the neo-cortex. We now know walnuts help develop more than three (3) dozen neuron-transmitters for brain function!

**Kidney beans** heal and help maintain kidney function, and yes, they look exactly like the human kidneys.

**Celery, bok choy, rhubarb, and many more** look just like bones. These foods specifically target bone strength. Bones are 23 percent sodium, and these foods are 23 percent sodium. If you do not have enough sodium in your diet, the body pulls it from the bones, thus making them weak. These foods replenish the skeletal needs of the body.

**Avocado, eggplant, and pears** target the health and function of the womb and cervix of the female, and they look like these organs. Research shows that when a woman eats one avocado a week, it balances hormones, sheds unwanted birth weight, and aids in the prevention of cervical cancer. And how profound is this? It takes exactly nine months to grow an avocado from blossom to ripen fruit. There are over fourteen thousand photolytic chemical constituents of nutrition in each one of these foods (modern science has only studied and named about 141 of them).

**Figs** are full of seeds and hang in twos when they grow. Figs increase the mobility of male sperm and increase the numbers of sperm as well to overcome male sterility.

**Sweet potatoes** look like the pancreas and help balance the glycemic index of diabetics.

**Olives** assist in the health and function of the ovaries. Another lookalike!

**Oranges, grapefruits, and other citrus fruits** look like the mammary glands of the female and assist the health of the breasts and the movement of lymph in and out of the breasts.

**Onions** look like the body's cells. Research shows that onions help clear waste materials from all the body's cells. They even produce tears, which wash the epithelial layers of the eyes. A working companion, **garlic**, also helps eliminate waste materials and dangerous free radicals from the body.

The old cliché "You are what you eat" does have merit. I am not saying that the above list of foods is a cure all. However, proper eating can prevent many of the ails we suffer from and there are natural foods and herbs that will absolutely replace many medicines (pills). Do some research and see what you find. Be an advocate for your own health.

Check out Proverbs 3 and have faith in God's pharmacy!

# It's All about "New"

*I*t's spring! As this season rolls in, we witness the splendor of God's love from the creation of the magnificent colors He provides for our eyes to see, and the sweet sounds of nature all around. Flowers are blooming. Green leaves are reappearing on the trees. Colorful birds' twerp and beautiful butterflies float through the air. Landscapes flaunt a colorful array of blossoming bushes and flowers—lavender, pink, yellow, red, and white! All these changes are indicative of the "new" spring season.

In addition to all the outside changes, the stores capture our attention with huge displays promoting chocolates, colored eggs, flowers, and the traditional Easter bunny.

These are all signs that Easter is approaching. Easter—the Christian holiday commemorating the crucifixion and Resurrection of our Lord and Savior, Jesus Christ. Easter—the holiday that we celebrate because of the privilege to have a Savior and the promise of everlasting life (John 3:16).

Easter baskets and Easter egg hunts are expectations that many children look forward to with excitement and anticipation. It means "goodies" and special treats are readily accessible!

Growing up, Easter was the one holiday that we got all "new" clothes. Everything was new. When we went to church on Easter Sunday, we donned a new hat, new dress or suit, white socks, patent leather shoes, and a new spring coat or cape. We even got "new" hairdos! We were always so excited about and proud of our new outfits. There are many fond memories of participating in the Easter plays at church and being "all dressed up." I do not recall any explanation as to why it was so important to our parents for us to have everything new, but it was a must! It was a little later in life that the realization that new outfits symbolized becoming new, getting rid of the old... (2 Corinthians 5:17).

While the new clothes were easily seen and visual, the change taking place internally was what really mattered. Without it being verbalized, we were taught self-confidence. We gained self-esteem. We learned to appreciate and be thankful for our parents and older siblings. Above all, we were taught and reminded that "God is good" and provides all our needs and much of our wants! We were taught to always thank and praise God for His goodness! We may not have totally understood the quiet teachings back then, but they planted deep roots.

Each day is a new beginning. As you begin each day with a smile and thankful heart, be ever mindful of the "newness" found only in Jesus Christ. Enjoy all the beauty around you. Take time to look at the sun, feel the breeze, listen to nature sounds, and enjoy those around you.

Celebrate this Easter season with praise and thanksgiving and make this commitment, "God, I am available to you. Use me!"

Happy Easter!

# Not Enough

*H*ave you ever been in a situation of not enough?
Perception is our reality. When we perceive not enough (true or not), it is where we are.

The not enough could be **not enough evidence** to convict when we are caught up in the justice system. Could be that evidence was destroyed, mishandled, or simply not present.

Although we all have the same number of hours in each given day, it may be **not enough time** to do all the things we hoped to do. Is this because we mismanage our time? Do we pile too many things on our plate for a given period?

When traveling, there are times when attempting to make hotel reservations or air travel, we find we have not accumulated enough points for a "freebie." **Not enough points** are disappointing. Do we look for another alternative?

There are days when there are chores to do, errands to run, and tasks that need completion, but there is just **not enough energy** to do it all. How do we handle it?

You are hoping for a promotion or applying for a new job and find that you do not meet the qualifications—**not enough education**! What do you do?

When attempting to pay bills, you realize there is **not enough money** to cover everything. What do you do? Have you been faithful in tithing? Have you been cheating God? What changes do you need to make with your finances?

We have a dog—Domino. Domino rarely gets enough to eat. Every day at mealtime, Domino sits and waits for us to finish eating. Then he makes two to three little barking snorts, asking for any leftovers. Once he gets those few crumbs, he goes back to his bowl to finish eating his food. That is his way of telling us, **his food alone is just not enough!**

You wake up in the morning and see the puffiness and bags under your eyes. Is this because of **not enough sleep,** or some other underlying condition?

Do you wake up concerned, stressed, and worried about life, health, and/or finances? Do you just not have **enough courage** to confront and deal with these issues? Do not let these worldly concerns rob you of your joy, peace, and prosperity. John 14:27 tells us, "Peace I leave with you; my peace I give you, I do not give to you as the world gives you. Do not let your hearts be troubled and do not be afraid."

Bottom line is this: Many of us can quote the Twenty-Third Psalms: "The LORD is my Shepherd; I shall not want…" **But** how many of us truly believe what we are saying, and stand firm in our faith that He will truly take care of us and meet our every need?

In all these situations of **not enough**, the scriptures tell us, "Blessed is he who trusts in the Lord" (Proverbs 16:20). "In all your ways acknowledge him, and he will make your paths straight" (Proverbs 3:6).

# Now Is the Time

*M*any of us are procrastinators in some phase of our lives. There are things we really don't enjoy doing, so we put them off. There are things that we don't feel confident about handling, so, we put them off. Nevertheless, almost daily we are posed with the question of when...

When am I going to start my diet?

When am I going to stop drinking?

When am I going to stop smoking?

When am I going to schedule that doctor's appointment for that much-needed physical exam?

When will I stop ignoring symptoms that are a warning of a potential health problem?

When will I stop being a hell-mate (belittling my mate), and become a helpmate?

When will I stop yelling at my children and start encouraging them and building their self-esteem?

When will I diligently do daily devotions and spend time praying for the sick, praying for my enemies and those who dislike me?

When will I open my heart and hands to give and to serve?

When will I sincerely seek God's will for my life?

The list goes on and on, and as usual, most of us say tomorrow, or as soon as...

That little word when can be such a burden, and a load that we don't have to carry.

We have all heard the cliché, "Let go and let God." Well, that applies to the "whens" in our lives and all the procrastinations. Today is not just a good day. Today is the best day to claim the scripture, "Praise be to the Lord, to God our Savior, who daily bears our burdens" (Psalm 68:19).

Imagine carrying a heavy bag of groceries up a steep flight of stairs, and the relief of reaching your destination and being able to put that bag down.

To rid ourselves of the when baggage, all we need to do is repent—change attitude and mind in respect to sin, God, and self. "In the past God overlooked such ignorance, but now he commands all people everywhere to repent" (Acts 17:30).

When...? Do not put off until tomorrow what can and should be done today! Now is the time!

# Oops! There It Is

*W*hat is happening to our world?

Where is the hope? Where is the joy?

We have one pandemic. Then we have a pandemic within a pandemic. We are experiencing a revival of protests along with the infiltration of mean-spirited agitators. The scriptures tell us, "If my people, who are called by my name, will humble themselves and pray and seek my face and turn from their wicked ways, then will I hear from heaven and will heal their land" (2 Chronicles 7:14). Are we there yet?

What will the new normal look like? Will there ever be a new normal?

Then as I read Ecclesiastes, I am reminded and convinced that only God can handle all this chaos. He will surely bring judgment—one day. This is just a season!

These are some of the questions many of us ask ourselves every day.

As I watch, read, and listen, I am amazed at the debauchery before us. I missed watching one of my favorite TV shows to hear the first presidential debate this week. That was precious time wasted, that I can never get back! However, listening to the two candidates, scriptures from Proverbs kept running through my mind. Here are just a few:

> "A chattering fool comes to ruin." (Proverbs 10:10)
>
> "Reckless words pierce like a sword, but the tongue of the wise brings healing." (Proverbs 12:18)

"When words are many, sin is not absent." (Proverbs 10:18)

"A wise man fears the Lord and shuns evil, but a fool is hotheaded and reckless." (Proverbs 14:16)

"A man of knowledge uses words with restraint, and a man of understanding is even-tempered. Even a fool is thought wise if he keeps silent…" (Proverbs 17:27–28)

"It is to a man's honor to avoid strife, but every fool is quick to quarrel." (Proverbs 20:3)

"A fool gives full vent to his anger, but a wise man keeps himself under control." (Proverbs 29:11)

"A fool shows his annoyance at once, but a prudent man overlooks an insult." (Proverbs 12:16)

Then this morning, as I watered and attended to my plants, there were new leaves and new sprouts in several of the pots. These plants are to me like pets are to many people. They make me happy. They do not talk back. They do not demand attention. They are just beautiful, green, and refreshing. Suddenly there was a moment of realization. Oops! There it is. The thriving and growing plant life in my home is a tangible and visual reminder that there is still joy. "Consider how the lilies grow. They do not labor or spin. Yet I tell you not even Solomon in all his splendor was dressed like one of these. If that is how God clothes the grass of the field, which is here today, and tomorrow is thrown into the fire, how much more will he clothe you…" (Luke 12:27). Oops! There it is.

# Opportunities to Be a Blessing

*E*very day I look around, and thankfully, I appreciate the splendor and wonder of creation and all the blessings the Savior provides. The fact that, the pantry is full, there is a roof over my head, and there is a clean, comfortable bed to sleep in, clean water to drink, and either heat or air to provide comfort—depending on the season. The reality is, most, if not all your needs are being met. You are tithing, volunteering, and giving all, you think you can give. If you are like me, many times, you may feel as though, I cannot possibly take on another thing, task, or project. Nevertheless, at that moment what may seem like an extra burden may be an awesome opportunity for you to be a blessing to someone and be blessed even more.

I have found that the tasks that I love have given me the opportunity to be a blessing. I love making quilts for Ronald McDonald House, so I set a goal to make several a year. Another enjoyable ongoing project is making personal care bags for the homeless and or needy. Becoming involved with Samaritan's Purse, making tote bags for the shoeboxes, and collecting items is another fantastic opportunity to bless those receiving the shoeboxes. Making pillowcase dresses for children in Africa provides yet another creative fun opportunity to be a blessing. Decorating the pillowcases and making each one special is very rewarding. Saving coins to help purchase water filters for Africa is another rewarding, ongoing project. Crocheting and knitting prayer shawls in a group setting, provides another way to form relationships, connect with a variety of people and bless.

You may think, busy, busy, expense, expense—yet it never ceases to amaze me that when God opens another door, expands my horizons, and finds something else to place in my heart and life, He provides the means to do so.

In 2015, due to some last-minute scheduling issues, I was approached about hosting a Pastor from India. Not having a host family for this pastor was causing a burden for my friend, so I agreed to share or try to eliminate this burden and be a host. Little did I know the abundant blessing I would receive. Rajendra Kumar, pastor of Sion Assembly Church, Vijayawada India, spent two weeks in our home and landed a permanent place in our hearts. Our family has now expanded to include his immediate family. Fortunately, we were able to meet his lovely wife and beautiful daughter and have daily talks—via Skype. So that even strengthened the bond. Hearing Pastor Rajendra's testimony, watching videos of the church services in India, seeing the slums, living conditions, and hearing that the average daily wage is about $10, and then seeing the orphanage and children they minister to and work with opened another place in my heart. Being very enamored by this young pastor, his works, the lives his ministries are touching, and the conditions in India, we opened our home for another visit this year to help with his mission to raise funds for the orphanage. He is spending another two weeks with us, and we are learning more about India, and how this ministry is growing and changing lives. It is wonderful! The orphanage has the capacity for two hundred children, but currently they only have the means to support twenty-four. They need help! If you have a desire to be a blessing to these orphan children, look up SAC Ministries www.sacministries.com and see what opportunities may be available to you and how you might be a blessing, and also read James 1:27.

# Organization 101

*W*hen it comes to your daily routine, what is the first thing you do each morning? Why is it important for you to do it?

Do you check your iPad and scan social media? How much time do you spend surfing the internet? How much time do you spend on Facebook—either posting or just reading? Then, during the day, how much of your day is spent texting or playing games? If you were to monitor that time, you would probably be amazed.

Maybe the morning newspaper is your thing. So you get the paper, scan it, check the obituaries, and then spend the next hour doing the crossword puzzles.

Do you put on music and leisurely enjoy a hot cup of coffee? You need the caffeine to jump start your day!

Perhaps you make a "to-do" list to get your day started. Many people do.

I vividly remember a lesson from Vacation Bible School when I was just a child. We were each given a Mason jar and some stones. The instructions were to put the stones in the jar identifying each task or job we needed or wanted to do that day. Each jar soon appeared to be full. Then we were given sand, and anxiously watched as the sand filled the gaps between the stones. We were all convinced that the jars were undoubtedly full. We were then given some water. To our surprise, the water worked its way between the stones and the sand. This illustration was to show us how easy it is to fill our day with "things," leaving little time for more important things in life—prayer and studying His Word.

How would this compare to your daily routine? Do you need to revisit Organization 101—first things first?

If all or some of these things take precedence over praying, reading, and studying His Word, then you possibly failed Organization 101. Let us start over. Check out these scriptures: "In all your ways acknowledge him, and he will make your paths straight" (Proverbs 3:6). Starting your day with an attitude of gratitude, praise, and thanksgiving is the first step to passing the course.

> "Study to show thyself approved unto God, a workman that needeth not to be ashamed, rightly dividing the word of truth." (2 Timothy 2:15)
>
> "Be joyful always: pray continually; give thanks in all circumstances..." (1 Thessalonians 5:16–18)
>
> "If my people, who are called by my name, will humble themselves and pray and seek my face and turn from their wicked ways, then will I hear from heaven and will forgive their sin and will heal their land." (2 Chronicles 7:14)

Organization 101 requires first things first!

# Poiema

*Poiema* is the Greek word for "workmanship" and translates as "masterpiece." The English words *poem* and *poetry* are derived from *poiema*. When I came across this word in one of my daily devotionals, it spoke to me.

We recently finished a wonderful series at church on "being a new creature in Christ." Pastor taught in depth on the positive advantages of a changed life. There is joy, power, comfort, and security when you are connected to the vine.

Then, I learned that a new book club was forming. Loving to read and learn, the thought of joining a book club was exciting. But it was even more exciting to learn that the name of the book club is "New Beginnings." Our first book was **The Paris Architect**, and that too was exciting. "New Beginnings" is such an appropriate name because this club promises new friendships, new surroundings, new opportunities to learn and share, and new beginnings in many aspects of our lives.

All this focus on "new" is not a coincidence. It is part of God' plan. It all ties together for me.

The word *poiema* popped into my life for a reason—to make me think profoundly about new. Think about being a new creature in Christ and how each of us should think of ourselves as a beautiful poem. The "New Beginnings" Book Club pulls together a group of people who find common interest in reading, discussing, and sharing. We share thoughts, opinions, ideas, and food! Our meeting place offers a safe environment where we can openly discuss and share our opinions and thoughts about the book, the characters, and the moral lesson of the book. "New Beginnings" reminds us to focus on the fact that our lives are designed to join and interlock to create a big picture, a great living tapestry woven of people and relationships. We are God's *poiema*—literally a poetic masterpiece made by God.

Sometimes we may get off track and not be able to see—for a minute—where we fit. But if we step back, take time to pray, be patient, and look at our life from His perspective—a scriptural view—we can see the overall masterpiece. If looking in this mirror is difficult or not clear, try talking directly to Him. You might say something like this:

> God help me to remember that I am your masterpiece—unique and beautiful as a poem. My identity rests in you!

After all, Ephesians 2:10 tells us, "For we are God's handiwork, created in Christ Jesus to do good works, which God prepared in advance for us to do."

Know that you are God's masterpiece—a valuable form of His creativity. Now go in confidence and do what He has planned for you to do—love one another, help one another, and serve where you can. You are blessed to bless! Let your light brightly shine so others may see that you are a new creature in Christ.

# P-O-T-E-N-T-I-A-L-I-T-Y

*O*ne of our favorite songs when my daughter was growing up was, "I Am a Promise."

When the youth choir belted out that song with such feeling and vibrancy, it made you smile for days. The lyrics to that song taught the youth that they were not an accident and that there were good things in store for them. There was a purpose for them being alive! We sang that song repeatedly, focusing on "I can be anything God wants me to be." We would literally take each line of the song and talk about it until there was no mistaking that, she was a promise.

The lyrics to "I Am a Promise" can be such a strong developmental guide for our youth. If parents would only take the time to instill in our young people that, there is a purpose for their lives. Just as the song says, "If you listen, you will hear His voice and if you are trying, He will help you." The key is to be still and listen for His direction and guidance.

The same is true for us grownups. Once we discover that each of us has the power within to release our potential, we are on our way to gratefulness! We gain the confidence to show strength, kindness, and compassion. The gratefulness that floods our hearts brings peace and harmony. To harness that "promise," "only believe."

The scriptures tell us we "are precious in His sight, and honored and loved" (Isaiah 43:4). So if we begin instilling, I am A Promise, in our babies, we will see positive results! Reading bedtime stories is great. But think about how awesome it would be to tuck the children in at night, or share with the older children at bedtime an affirmation that you place them in God's care and keeping, and that His presence guards and protects them. The seed is planted!

Teaching our children to be positive about life and that anything is attainable makes the child strive harder to be all that he/she can be. Having the confidence to put aside limiting beliefs, helps them eliminate the "I can't" from their vocabulary bank. That is a good thing!

Joseph Campbell once said, "The meaning of life is whatever you ascribe it to be. Being alive is the meaning." Keeping that quote in mind and focusing on the scriptures, embrace what being a promise means and teach all our children that, "I am a child of God, on a divinely directed path of good—a unique and personal path." Teach them "I am a promise." Teach them "I am a potentiality." Teach them that they can be anything they want to be, and at night, reiterate the promise and p-o-t-e-n-t-i-a-l-i-t-y!

As the scriptures say, "Train a child in the way he should go, and when he is old, he will not turn from it" (Proverbs 22:6).

Teach them to claim the promise and when they rise in the morning, start the day with the song, "Rise, Shine, Give God the Glory." It worked for us. Try it for yourself!

# Prayer Saved My Life

*H*ave you ever been in a situation and did not know how you were going to make it through? Suddenly, the worst was over, and your feet were back on solid ground. How did this happen? Why did it happen? Have you considered that someone is and was praying for you?

A few years ago, a tornado touched down in the area. We witnessed devastation all around. Trees were uprooted. Roofs were blown off. Power was off for days. Yet our home was unscathed. We had power. Plants that were on the deck were still standing and the porch furniture was all in place. I believe we are on someone's prayer list!

Do you recall the accident of the tractor-trailer that lost control as it was traveling on Interstate 79 near the Meadowbrook exit a few years ago? That huge vehicle rolled over the railing during a busy time of the day, landed on Johnson Avenue and there was not one fatality. It did not even damage one car! How was that possible? Someone was praying!

A few months a very good friend had a surgery that incapacitated her for several weeks. There was great concern on how she would manage daily necessities, activities, and meals for her and her elderly husband. Prayer interceded. Another friend with "spiritual" binoculars, made contacts with other friends and coordinated arrangements for the delivery of daily meals and other needed services. It all worked out beautifully. Prayer changes things!

As a child, I remember tumbling down the sixteen front porch steps landing on a concrete stoop, and only had a busted lip. That could easily have been a fatal fall. However, I believe someone was praying for me.

I am also remembering lying on slats in a hospital room—in and out of consciousness. Could not move due to the multiple injuries—which included a broken hip and crushed pelvis. Overheard the doctors talking, and the orthopedic doctor was saying he would do surgery and insert pins and rods that would make me more comfortable, but I would never be able to walk again. I just could not grasp that diagnosis and I refused the surgery. Consequently, I lay paralyzed for about five months. Then one day, there was movement in my legs. Intensive therapy got me to crutch in about a month and the rest is history! Someone was praying for me. Those prayers changed my life!

I am remembering being hit broad side by a speeding car when I was seven months pregnant. The car was a total loss, but I only had a seat belt bruise! Once again, I know PRAYER covered me!

Take a few minutes, hush, relax, and think about all the near misses you have encountered. Can you even begin to count the number of times prayer saved your life? What about the storms He has brought you through? Do you know who might have been praying and interceding for you?

The telephone is ringing as you are about to leave for an appointment. You hesitate in answering—but you do. The call lasts too long—in your opinion. However, just a few minutes delay prevented you from being involved in a major traffic accident.

Before getting in any vehicle is a wonderful time to pray—not only for yourself but also for all you may encounter on your travels. The scriptures tell us to "pray without ceasing." Moreover, the seclusion of your auto is fertile grounds for prayer—silently or aloud.

Psalms 33:20 tells us, "We wait in hope for the Lord; he is our help and our shield."

I have been on someone's prayer list for as long as I can remember. And I have no doubt that those prayers have carried me thus far. Prayer saved me and saved my life!

Who are you praying for?

# Putting Things in Perspective

*D*o you need that pair of shoes you saw on sale? How many pairs of shoes are in your closets that have only been worn once, or maybe never? You say, they too were on sale, and you thought you might have an outfit they matched—and you did not—so they are just sitting there. Have you given any thought to the number of women, men, and children who have no shoes and out of necessity go bare foot each day? How many people could you make happy by cleaning out your shoe inventory? There are several mission groups looking for new or slightly worn shoes to send to those in need. Look for one of these groups and donate.

Take a brief survey of your kitchen. Are there utensils, cookware, or dishes that are just there taking up space because you attended a "cooking party" and just had to buy something? If you are not using it, give it to someone who can, and will use it. That will take care of some clutter and help someone in need or at least make someone happy.

Take a walk to the garage. Could you park a second car in there if you got rid of all your accumulations that are being stored—just in case you might need them? Perhaps, you are keeping all these **things**, because you have been thinking about a possible garage sale—for the last three or four years—that has never happened. Why keep them?

If there was a fire and your home was destroyed, would making an inventory of all your lost possessions be next to impossible? If you have been holding on to **things** for years, where you even begin to start with the inventory? Do you even know what is in your closets, drawers, garage, or under the beds?

Jesus lived and taught that life does not consist in the accumulation of things—Luke 12. While He is not the typical picture of a homeless man, think about this—he somehow managed to survive three years of ministry—travel included without owning anything except the clothes on His back, for all we know!

When we travel, it's cosmetics, swimsuits, swimsuit cover-ups, matching shoes for several different outfits, several changes of underwear, etc.... Do we need it all? How many things do you bring back home from a trip that you never wore? And the thought is, "I guess I overpacked this time." Truth is that might be a sign that you just have way more than you need and it is time to share!

Take a few moments to think about all the possessions you are holding on to for no real good reason. Pray about why you have so much and what you should do with it all and then...

Take a faith step—clean a closet today and get rid of unnecessary things. Donate anything of worth and toss the insignificant. You may be surprised how large a garbage bag you need and how good it feels to declutter!

Think about Acts 2:45: "Selling their possessions and goods, they gave to anyone as he had need."

# Recall Notice

*It* seems that almost daily some automobile manufacturer posts a recall notice. There may be a feature on the vehicle that has a dangerous or perhaps fatal component, and the only prevention is a recall. It might also be a part that does not function as previously thought. At any rate some action must be taken to alleviate potential problems and or danger. There are eight hundred numbers to call or a list of steps to go through to correct the problem.

The food industry is also notorious for recalls. If there is not some type of pathogen or death threatening bacteria lurking in one of our foods, there has been some mishandling that poses a danger. This is also handled by a recall and a warning—do not use!

Filed in my "stash" was the following article about a "recall" that we should all be mindful.

The Maker of all human beings (GOD) is recalling all units manufactured, regardless of make or year, due to a serious defect in the primary and central component of the heart.

This is due to a malfunction in the original prototype units code named Adam and Eve, resulting in the reproduction of the same defect in all subsequent units. This defect has been identified as "subsequent internal nonmorality," more commonly known as SIN.

Some of the symptoms include the following:

- Loss of direction
- Foul vocal emissions
- Amnesia of origin
- Lack of peace and joy
- Selfish or violent behavior

- Depression or confusion
- Fearfulness
- Idolatry
- Rebellion

The Manufacturer, who is neither liable nor at fault for this defect, is providing factory-authorized repair and service free of charge to correct this defect. The Repair Technician, **JESUS**, has most generously offered to bear the entire burden of the staggering cost of these repairs. There is no additional fee required. The number to call for repair in all areas is **P-R-A-Y-E-R**. Once connected, please upload your burden of **SIN** through the **REPENTANCE** procedure. Next, download **ATONEMENT** from the Repair Technician, **JESUS**, into the heart component.

No matter how big or small the **SIN** defect is, **JESUS** will replace it with the following:

- Love
- Joy
- Peace
- Patience
- Kindness
- Goodness
- Faithfulness
- Gentleness
- Self-Control

Please see the operating manual, the BIBLE (*best instructions before leaving Earth*) for further details on the use of these fixes.

Warning: Continuing to operate the human being without correction voids any manufacturer warranties, exposing the unit to dangers and problems too numerous to list, and will result in the human unit permanently impounded. For free emergency service, call on JESUS.

Danger: The human being units not responding to this recall action will have to be scrapped in the furnace. The SIN defect will not be permitted to enter Heaven so as to prevent contamination of the facility. Thank you for your attention.

PS: Please assist where possible by notifying others of this important recall notice, and you may contact the Father anytime by "knee mail"!

"Pray continually" (1 Thessalonians 5:17).

# Reflecting on the Legacy of Dr. Martin Luther King Jr.

*I*n 1983, President Ronald Regan signed a bill that named the third Monday in January a holiday in observance of Martin Luther King Jr.'s birthday. Since that time, churches, schools, civic organizations, libraries, and other groups take time to acknowledge the footprint that this great civil rights leader left on this country and the world.

Most often programs and ceremonies refer to his speeches and the impact of his well-worded metaphors. In one of his most profound speeches delivered on April 3, 1968, he told the audience: "I have seen the Promised Land. I may not get there with you. But I want you to know tonight, that we as a people, will get to the Promised Land." The very next day he was assassinated.

Dr. King's legacy, philosophy, actions, and life is the epitome of the love we read about in 1 Corinthians 13.

While celebrations take place around the third week in January, Dr. King was born January 15, 1929, and named Michael King Jr., after his father, who was a Baptist minister. In 1934, Michael King Sr. went on a missionary trip and tour of Rome, Tunisia, Egypt, Jerusalem, Bethlehem, and Berlin. In Berlin, he witnessed the racial animosity, oppression, and unfair treatment toward the Jews, people of color and other subjects, and the stand that Martin Luther and the Protestants were taking. The impact was so great that when he returned home, Michael king Sr. changed his name to Martin Luther in honor of the great protestant leader Martin Luther. He also changed his son's name to Martin Luther King Jr. However, it was not until July 23, 1957, when MLK Jr. was twenty-eight years old that an official birth certificate change was made.

Growing up, Dr. King had plans to become a doctor or a lawyer; however, he was not able to escape the many profound truths he found in the scriptures. He skipped grades 9 and 12 and entered Morehouse College at the age of fifteen. He then entered the Crozer Theological Seminary in Pennsylvania, graduating with his PhD at the age of twenty-five. He also attended Boston University.

It is interesting that during his first year at seminary he got only a C in public speaking. He either stepped up his game or had different instructors; because by his final year he was receiving straight As and had become the valedictorian of his class.

In 1964, at the age of thirty-five, Dr. King won the Nobel Peace Prize. He was the youngest person to do so. Malala Yousafzai now holds that record, winning the 2014 prize at age seventeen.

Nelson Mandela in 2014 said, "No one truly knows a nation until one has been inside its jails. A nation should not be judged by how it treats its highest citizens, but its lowest ones. Prison itself is a tremendous education in the need for patience and perseverance." Dr. King was jailed twenty-nine times, often on trumped up charges—driving thirty miles per hour in a 25mph zone in Alabama! These infractions were not DUIs (driving under the influence), but what now is commonly referred to as DWB (driving while Black).

Dr. Martin Luther King Jr. is the only person born in these United States whose birthday is a federal holiday. George Washington was born before the United States came to be.

In John 7:24 we find these words, "Stop judging by mere appearances, and make a right judgment." Are we yet inching in that direction?

"For there is no difference between Jew and Gentile—the same Lord is Lord of all and richly blesses all who call on Him" (Romans 10:9).

Think on this, another of Dr. King's quotes: "Life's most persistent and urgent question is, "What are you doing for others?"

Truly Dr. Martin Luther King was a great leader and example for us all.

# Renaissance of the Clarksburg Community

*O*h, happy day! Clarksburg is being revitalized. There are major renovations and new construction taking place all over the city. I hope that the beautification restores positive activity and enthusiasm, not only within the city but also in all the surrounding area.

Back in the day, the Kelly Miller School Building, located on Water Street (recently renamed E. B. Saunders Way), was one of the bright spots in the community. Completed in 1919, the school opened to serve as the educational institution for the Black student population of Harrison, Lewis, Barbour, and Taylor counties. Occasionally youth from Tucker and Clay County were able to find lodging in the area and be a part of the Kelly Miller program. The school was named after Kelly Miller, a nationally noted intellectual, originally from Winnsboro, NC. The famed Kelly Miller was a Dean at Howard University with a background in mathematics and social work and was a journalist.

E. B. Saunders named first principal of the school, served in that capacity until 1956. Professor D. H. Kyle, with a master's degree in Latin, and a strong proponent of Afrocentric studies, taught Latin, and history, and served as Dean.

The school was equipped with an auditorium seating approximately six hundred, a full-size gymnasium, a swimming pool, science labs, and a large cafeteria.

The building also served as a cultural center, offering stage plays, musicals, and top-notch sports programs.

After the integration of schools, the Kelly Miller School Building remained vacant for several years.

In an effort to recognize the man, the school, the community, and keep alive the wonderful memories and history of the school, the alumni of the school formed the Kelly Miller Foundation in 1985. The primary focus of the Foundation was providing scholarships to Afro-American students pursuing higher education.

The Harrison County Board of Education (BOE) moved into the Kelly Miller Building in the mid-eighties and after several "good" years at that location, the BOE was afforded the opportunity to relocate to a prime spot in the center of the city—thanks to Dominion Resources. Early in 2017, The Kelly Miller building was donated to the West Virginia Black Heritage Festival (WVBHF). The WVBHF in collaboration with the Monticello Ongoing Revitalization Project (MORE) is striving to revitalize the building and establish The Kelly Miller Community Center.

Plans are to offer services and programs, at one location, that are beneficial to the entire community. For this to happen, we must get back to the basics. That means community members must become and stay involved with this project. We must start volunteering our time, talents, and perhaps our finances to accomplish this effort. We must become our brother's keepers, as was done years ago. If you witness wrongdoing, or injustices occurring, use that cell phone and dial 911. Be part of the solution, not part of the problem.

It is said that things come full circle. The Kelly Miller Building is once again aimed at being a vital, active part of the community—serving youth as well as adults. It is time for the community to take back the reigns of the community. Get involved. Stay involved. Let us make the Kelly Miller Community Center a project we can all be proud to say, "I was a part of that."

# Repeat Offenders

$\mathcal{A}$ s a society, we tend to be familiar with and accustomed to punishment for repeat offenders. In the sports arena, everyone knows that in baseball, three strikes mean the batter is out. Since the batter was not able to make contact with the baseball, the team is at a standstill, and can't move forward until the next batter takes the plate. After three outs, the opposing team gets the opportunity to try and score. So 3 is the magic number for punishment and change in baseball.

Our court system did a piggy-back on baseball's three—strike rule and in 1993 passed a "three-strikes" law. This law significantly increased prison time for persons convicted of a felony. After two convictions, a person is considered a repeat offender and a menace to society. Therefore, under the "three-strikes" law, a third conviction carries a mandatory prison sentence of twenty years to life. This means one would be incarcerated for at least twenty years before they would even be eligible for parole. California wasted no time and implemented this law in 1994. By 2004, twenty-six states had some form of "three-strikes" law in place, and now that number reaches twenty-eight. Georgia, South Carolina, and Tennessee even have "two-strike" laws for serious violent crimes. That tell me that extradition to these states could easily be fatal. "Three-strikes" is/was intended to be a deterrent for repeat offenders. Questions we might ask ourselves are, is "three strikes" working? Has the court case load declined? Have the felonies and crime rates declined? Why are we building more prisons? Are our communities safer?

A concern with the "three-strike" law, is that if you belong to a certain socioeconomic class and have the financial means you receive preferential treatment. This means the third strike, for the privileged, could and often is "treatment" in lieu of a life sentence. An example of that would be Robert Downey Jr. and his convictions due to his habitual drug issues. Think about that!

If we are honest with ourselves, many of us are or have been repeat offenders. We commit the same offenses repeatedly. We may overindulge at the dinner table on a regular basis. We may commit lustful or immoral acts frequently. We might be carrying the baggage of unforgiveness. Out of our mouths flow unkind and crude language. Then some of us have allowed kings and idols (money, cars, houses, things) to be dominant in our world. Do you realize how fortunate we are that God does not have a "three-strike" law? If He did, where would we be?

Are you a repeat offender? Have you ever been a repeat offender? You may recall a time in your life when you struck out—three strikes, but God says, "I, even I, am He who blots out your transgressions, for my own sake, and remembers your sins no more" (Isaiah 43:25). No Judge, lawyer or courtroom is needed. He has your back!

> "If you return to the Lord, then your brothers and your children will be shown compassion by their captors...for the LORD your God is gracious and compassionate. He will not turn His face from you if you return to Him." (2 Chronicles 30:9)
>
> "In Him we have redemption through his blood, the forgiveness of sins, in accordance with the riches of God's grace that He lavished on us with all wisdom and understanding." (Ephesians 1:7–8)

Repeat offenders, let us all praise and thank God that He does not have a "three-strike" rule for us!

# Roots

$\mathcal{T}$he word *root* has several meanings, and it depends on the conversation and the context as to how the word is interpreted. From an agricultural view, a discussion of roots would be about the underground portion of a plant that serves as support and draws food and water from the surrounding soil. Root could also refer to the embedded part of an organ or structure such as hair, tooth, or nerve.

Several years ago, *Roots* was a popular movie and series about African ancestry.

In mathematics, the word *root* has several meanings, depending on the application you are doing.

In the world of foreign languages, Latin is not as popular as French or Spanish, but Latin was and is great for the deciphering the meaning of words. Knowing Latin root words is also a great asset in spelling and word games.

The Bible is also a root for many clichés we regularly use when many of us don't even realize we are being biblical. Some examples are as follows:

- Engage brain before putting mouth in gear, or putting your foot in your mouth has roots from Proverbs 10:19: "When words are many, sin is not absent, but he who holds his tongue is wise." Also in Ecclesiastes 5:2–3, we find these words: "Be not rash with thy mouth, and let not thine heart be hasty to utter anything: therefore let thy words be few.... A fool's voice is known by multitude of words.
- Take it easy, I have got this. "Be still, and know that I am God…" (Psalms 46:10).

- The road to hell is paved with good intentions. St. Bernard of Clairvaux in the tenth century said it this way: "Hell is full of good intentions or desires." Proverbs 16:17 says, "The highway of the upright is to depart from evil; he that keepeth his way preserveth his soul."
- Want to make God laugh—make your own plans. In Proverbs 19:21 (NIV) we find these words, "Many are the plans in a person's heart, but it is the Lord's purpose that prevails."
- Somehow, we'll make it. Everything will be all right. "Trust in the Lord with all thine heart: lean not unto thine own understanding. In all thy ways acknowledge him, and he shall direct thy paths" (Proverbs 3:5–6). Also, check out Psalms 37:23–26.
- Words must be weighed, not counted. "The words of the wise are like goads, their collected sayings like firmly embedded nails—given by one Shepherd" (Ecclesiastes 12:11).
- Write your sorrow in the sand, and your blessings in stone. "The blessings of the Lord bring wealth, and he adds no trouble to it" (Proverbs 10:22).
- The more we work at what we should be, the less we will need to hide what we are. "Create in me a pure heart, O God; and renew a right spirit within me" (Psalms 51:10).

This is my opinion of just a few examples of sayings that I find the Bible as the root source. Therefore, if you use clichés, you would be wise to search for the root. If you find that root in the scriptures, you know it is an absolute truth. Check for roots and be confident in Proverbs 3:5–6.

# See Something, Do Something

How do you respond when you see a need? Are you quick to offer a prayer—that may never be prayed—and move on, thinking you have said the right words?

Think about how you handle or mishandle issues or someone else's needs. Are you generous in responding to a need, or are you selfish—thinking only about self?

There are many sayings that make one stop and think about how they might be handling life. One of my favorites is "If you want to make God laugh, make your own plans." Another is "The road to hell is paved with good intentions." Remember, do not put off until tomorrow what you can do today. Why? You may not be here to see tomorrow! That is fact—not fiction!

Try this one on for size, "If you want to make God smile, be obedient to His Word."

Daily we hear about and witness or encounter many of life's troubles. Whether it is personal or somewhat distant, turbulence, confusion, stress, economic uncertainty, racial division, physical and emotional pain, dreadful diseases, addictions, or threats of war, invades our life on some level. Often, we are so busy or in such a hurry, that it is easy for us to keep moving and not take time to listen to what God may be telling us to do. You might be able to satisfy a need just by being a "good listener." You may be able to provide a simple act of kindness, or just give a pat on the back. Your attention or companionship might just save a life.

Prayer is GREAT, and I truly believe prayer changes things; however, the immediate need might be a hamburger. Are you willing to go that route? You might surprise yourself by what you have that you can share without much of a sacrifice. The need might be for a pair of gloves, and you probably have three or four more pair at home. Give up the gloves!

If you see a need, please do something. Think about the biblical story of Ruth and Naomi. Ruth saw that Naomi was aging, alone and needed her companionship. Her vow to stay with Naomi proved to be most beneficial for both. Ruth saw a need, and she did something!

God has called us to be part of a community. We should bear the responsibilities of that calling. There is peace in communion with others and helping those in need. So if you see a need, do something!

If you don't have the resources to help, consider a referral to the Clarksburg Mission, Hope for Domestic Violence, Shepherd's Corner, Mustard Seed, Health Access or perhaps check for a list of one of the other United Way Agencies.

"Trust in the Lord and do good..." (Psalm 37:3).

One small act of kindness could change the trajectory of someone's life, and possibly yours also.

# Seize the Day

*E*ach morning after prayer, and before starting my daily routine of devotional readings, I retrieve and read my laminated copy of the following prayer by Helen Steiner Rice:

> Good Morning, God
> You are ushering in another day
> Untouched and freshly new,
> So here I come to ask You, God,
> If you'll renew me too?
> Forgive the many errors that
> I made yesterday,
> And let me try again, dear God,
> To walk closer in Thy way.
> But Father, I am well aware
> I can't make it on my own,
> So take my hand and hold it tight
> For I can't walk alone.

Although I know the prayer by heart, reading it somehow sets the stage for the day ahead.

During the pandemic that we are currently experiencing, each day seems to signal that a new normal is pending. What is next?

Time has a way of seemingly flying by, and things, situations, and people change almost instantly. The day that lies ahead of you—or the one you just finished—may be stormy and overcast, or bright and sunny. Whatever the case, this day is a precious gift from God.

This gift amounts to 86,400 seconds. Have you used one of those seconds to say, "Thank you?"

How many times have you heard, "Mañana—I'll do it tomorrow?"

How many times have you said, "Mañana—I'll do it tomorrow?"

Why is it that we procrastinate and postpone? Is it because something is unfavorable? Is it because we do not believe we can actually accomplish the task before us? Perhaps you think if you wait, someone will do it for you. Whatever!

Bottom line: Time is irreplaceable and more valuable than money. Tomorrow is not promised, and you may not live to see mañana. Seize this day! Now is the right time. Do not let age stop your creative juices from flowing. Do not think you're too young for things to happen, or too old to achieve. Do not wait for a moment that may never happen. Seize this day! "Take no thought for the morrow: for the morrow shall take thought for the things of itself..." (Matthew 6:34).

Call a friend who has been on your mind. Send a "thinking of you" card. Plan that beach vacation. Purge that "overstuffed" closet or drawers—and donate the good stuff to a nonprofit or share with a relative or friend. Once this day is gone, it will never return. That gift of 86,400 seconds does not fall under the thirty-day return policy. Seize this day to live, love and serve. Know that every day, every breath is a reason to celebrate and say, "Thank You, Father." Seize the day!

# "Shake, Rattle, and Roll"

"Shake, Rattle, and Roll" is the title of a popular, controversial song recorded on Atlantic Records in the mid-1950s. Joe Turner did the original version. Bill Haley, Bill Haley and the Comets, and the famous idol, Elvis Pressley, all recorded slightly different versions of that song during the same period. The song had a catchy tune, but we were not allowed to sing that song in our home, and being kids, we could not understand why. All we knew was that it seemed to be a good song for dancing. We thought the lyrics were about dancing and having a good time. It wasn't until much later in life that I listened closely to the words and realized the sexual overtone of the lyrics. Then, I knew why my parents were so adamant about not listening to or singing that song. If they were alive today, much of the popular music would undoubtedly be taboo. They would be appalled about the "popular" songs of this day and the lyrics that the youth know so well and are openly singing!

Forgetting about the lyrics of "Shake, Rattle, and Roll," the title is clearly, what we need to consider about THINGS in our lives. Shake, rattle, and roll! The habits, the people, the addictions, the abuse, and any other thing that is keeping us from getting closer to God, we must get the courage to shake, rattle, and roll!

Having misunderstandings with friends or family members and carrying a grudge rather than being humble and trying to reconcile and settle the differences is a waste of precious time. Saying I am sorry if I offended you, allows you to get beyond the petty differences and mend hurt feelings. Shake, rattle, and roll! Life is too short to harbor bad feelings.

If you are hanging with folks that are having a negative influence on your life, and keeping you from reaching your potential, you need to let them go. Tell them you are moving forward and do it! Shake, rattle, and roll!

That habit that is interfering with your walk, admit what it is and that it is wrong, seek help, and move on. Shake, rattle, and roll!

*Woman Thou Art Loosed*, a book authored by Pastor T. D. Jakes could easily have been subtitled *Shake, Rattle, and Roll*. The same basic theory applies—that there is freedom in letting go and letting God and moving on with your life in a positive environment and manner.

Listening to people complain about the churches they attend and how unsatisfied they are is distressing. Attending a church where you are not being fed and growing is unnecessary. David Wilkerson has said, "diluted gospel is no gospel at all." Diluted gospel is messages that seek to please men rather than please God. You know about this type of preaching/teaching. If you are in this type of environment you must Shake, Rattle and Roll. In your heart, you know when it is time to shake the dust off your feet and move on. Do not let traditions, laziness, or habit keep you from your blessings and happiness. There is a church for you. "Seek and you shall find."

We all know that cancer is a dreaded disease. Cancer is a disease we all fear. When we hear stage 4 cancer, we immediately almost lose hope. That news is most frightening. Staying a slave to THINGS that keep you from moving closer to God is just like cancer to your soul. These THINGS, like cancer, will slowly but surely eat away your life! Think about these THINGS, pray, and fast about these THINGS, and shake, rattle, and roll! While making up your mind to shake, rattle, and roll read Matthew 10:14 and Acts 18:6. Then, just do it!

# Shared Burdens Travel Lighter

We are in a pandemic within a pandemic. COVID-19 is new. Oppression, injustice, and blatant disregard for human life is ancient!

Examine our *now*!

In 1953, a statue was sculpted and placed in the center of our town, Clarksburg, staunchly, memorably, and as I have been told specifically to intimidate the Black community. It was a reminder of who was at the top of the food chain. This overt gesture is and always will be, a reminder of systematic racism, segregation, slavery, and injustice. While many of us want to move beyond those times, unfortunately, there are too many that still entertain and want to hold fast to times of past and the status that they held.

In 1991, when we contemplated moving to this area, I did not even notice the statue at the courthouse. I was impressed because I saw a church on nearly every corner. In retrospect, one cannot help but wonder, what were/are these churches teaching? What scriptures were people hiding in their hearts so they would not sin against God? (Psalm 119:10–11). Perhaps, "Create in me a clean heart, O God; and renew a steadfast spirit within me" (Psalms 51:10) was not fully digested.

Let us review His Words:

> Genesis 1:26–28: We are equally made in God's image.
> Proverbs 22:6: Train a child in the way he should go—do not teach hate.
> Romans 2:11: God does not have favoritism.

John 13:15: Follow the example Jesus set." Do as
   I have done unto you."
Mark 12:31: Love your neighbor as yourself.
James 2:1–4: Do not discriminate and judge with
   evil thoughts.
Galatians 3:26–29: We are **all** sons of God
   through faith in Jesus Christ.

These scriptures in no way confirm that we are all the same. But we are all equal in God's sight and He loves each of us—rich, poor, Black, White, or whatever!

It appears that too many churches and church leaders not only tolerate racism and division, by enthusiastically and proudly welcoming the wealthy and certain ethnicities, while doing outreach to the poor and disenfranchised—making sure to keep the undesirables at a distance.

There is a movie now trending, *The Same Kind of Different as Me*. Watching it just might help give a wholesome picture of someone that looks different than you. Their differences may even make you uncomfortable, but beyond your natural vision, look with your heart.

We have lost so much of our true history through inadequate teaching, misrepresentation, tradition without deep explanation and textbooks that only tell the bits and pieces of the story. We have succumbed to ignorance, pride, resistance to change, and teaching our children to hate, so much so, that these things have filled hearts and minds, superseding, and replacing biblical truths.

Proverbs 4:14 plainly tells us, "Enter not into the path of the wicked, and go not in the way of evil men." What path are you following or promoting?

The oppressive institutions like systematic racism, are wrong. In the very first book of the Bible, slavery and oppression are depicted. The story of Joseph, and the mistreatment by his brothers resulted in Joseph being in slavery. It took Joseph twenty-two years to gain his freedom. But once free, he was free indeed! Although the Emancipation Proclamation was signed in 1862, people of color continue to struggle to truly be free. The struggle is real. Oppression and injustice have lasted much too long.

"Now the Lord is the Spirit, and where the Spirit of the Lord is, there is freedom" (2 Corinthians 3:17). Is the Lord not present in these United States of America?

"Finally, brothers, whatever is true, whatever is noble, whatever is right, whatever is pure, whatever is lovely, whatever is admirable—if anything is excellent or praiseworthy-think about such things" (Philippians 4:8).

"If my people, who are called by my name, will humble themselves and pray and seek my face and turn from their wicked ways, then will I hear from Heaven and will forgive their sin and will heal their land" (2 Chronicles 7:14).

What can or will you do to help the situation?

Shared burdens make way for peace and lighter loads.

# Shattered Vessels

*S* *hattered Vessels* is the title of a very interesting and intriguing novel written by Nancy Flowers. Research will show several books and titles related to this topic; however, this is the one with which I am familiar.

This author, Nancy Flowers, visited and participated in the WV Black Heritage Festival several years ago, and I had the opportunity to meet her and converse with her about her writings. Consequently, I purchased this novel and another one of her books, *A Fool's Paradise*, along with beautiful posters depicting the novels. These posters are now framed and have a home, along with other art, in my daughter's apartment.

Having the opportunity to spend time at my daughter's and see these posters daily, served as a reminder of the real-life situations so many women face daily. The *Shattered Vessel* poster portrays images of a diverse group of women, clearly showing that abuse can affect anyone. The poster is a very attractive, yet disturbing piece of art, if you take time to analyze it, or look deep into the troubled faces.

The novel focuses on abuse and the volatile situations so many victims find themselves in. Questions posed by the author are real ones that can serve as pivotal points for all of us.

- When is it okay for a man to raise his hand, fist, or any other object at his spouse or significant other? The answer is NEVER.
- When is it acceptable to belittle, disrespect, cheat or neglect your significant other? The answer, once again, is NEVER.

- And most importantly, when should one remain in an abusive relationship without serious intervention and therapy? NEVER!

We, as women, must learn to love ourselves enough to put ourselves first and become untangled in the abuse cycle.

Finally, the author proclaims, "Women, realize your power. Woman is Mother Earth. We bear and give life to the flowers in bloom today and tomorrow. Love yourself enough to put you first!"

All that this author shares and tries to instill in us was so eloquently and profoundly presented by T. D. Jakes, renown pastor and motivational speaker, in a seminar I was blessed to attend. Pastor Jakes took a twenty-dollar bill, crumbled it, tore off a piece, stomped on it, spit on it, and practically mutilated it, while proclaiming its still current value. That $20 bill represented an abused woman, still alive and still valuable. That seminar had a profound impact on my life and left a lasting impression.

Knowing that abuse is so widespread and potentially deadly, look for ways to help and show compassion to these victims. If you witness immediate danger, do not hesitate to dial 911. If you want to be more personally supportive, contact HOPE Coalition Against Domestic Violence, and see how you might serve.

Shattered vessels are everywhere. Let us be the glue to help put them back together.

If you happen to be the victim, the lyrics to the song, "The Potter's House," has a message for you.

The Potter's House

In case you have fallen by the wayside of life;
  Dreams and visions shattered, and
You are broken inside. You don't have to stay in
  the shape you're in
The Potter wants to put you back together again.

In case your situation has turned upside down,
    and all that you have accomplished is now
    on the ground,
You don't have to stay in the shape that you're in.
The Potter wants to put you back together again.
You who are broken, stop by the Potter's House.
You who need mending, stop by the Potter's
    House.
Give Him the fragments of your broken life.
My friend, the Potter wants to put you back
    together again.
There's Joy in the Potter's House.
There's Peace in the Potter's House.
There's Love in the Potter's House.
There's Salvation in the Potter's House.
There's Healing in the Potter's House.
There's Deliverance in the Potter's House.
You'll find everything you need in the Potter's
    House.
The Potter wants to put you back together again.
    Womb.

"You created my inmost being; You knit
me together in my mother's womb. I praise You
because I am fearfully and wonderfully made…"
(Psalms 139:13–14).

# Shifting Gears

*A*nyone who has ever had the opportunity or challenge to drive a stick-shift vehicle can relate to the following comparison. For the past few months, we have all been shifting gears dealing with the current pandemic of COVID-19. We hit the starter; depress the clutch while shifting from neutral to first gear. We gain a little momentum; slowly depress clutch again so we can shift to second gear. Finally, the momentum is there and once again, you slowly depress the clutch so you can shift to third gear. If you can maintain the speed, third gear will take you a long way. If you just slow down however, you may be able to go back to second gear and then right back to third. However, if you come to a stop, the whole process must start all over again.

In February, the Coronavirus made its appearance—the starter. Although some warnings and cautions were issued, many did not take things seriously—neutral. Then came the quarantine—first gear. Second gear—quarantine, masks, and safe distancing.

Third gear—masks, safe distancing, and trying to resume previous activities, and reopen businesses, etc. This period is lasting longer than anyone initially could have anticipated. Stops (disobedience) and bumps have resulted in shifting gears once again.

When I was a teenager, learning to drive, my father insisted I learn to drive a stick shift. At first, he took me to a large field or the school parking lot after school hours. He had me practice starting, shifting gears, and stopping. That was easy and fun. After a while, when he would take me practice driving, he would intentionally go to a hilly area, and make me stop midway up a steep hill, so I would learn how to shift gears without slipping backward. Initially, this was so frightening and made me very nervous. And yes, there were some tears! Daddy did not seem to care that there were three pedals—gas pedal, clutch, and the brake—and I only had two small feet! That was a hard situation to grasp. At some point, my fears subsided, and I was able to master shifting gears, on a hill, without stripping the clutch and without sliding backward.

Although not quite the same, think about the man at the pool of Bethesda. For thirty-eight years, he lingered at the side of the pool waiting for someone to help him. But when Jesus told him, "Stand up, take your mat and walk," the man shifted (gears) his belief in his limitations, freed himself and was healed (John 5:8).

The woman at the well inched forward—shifted gears—just enough to touch the hem of Jesus's garment and was healed.

What stopped the man at the Bethesda pool from doing the same thing? Was it fear? Was it worry about rejection? Or was it lack faith?

When I let go of my shifting fears, and concentrated on coordination, I was able to drive on smoothly!

What is limiting your progress? Is lack of confidence, fear, or lack of faith?

While there seem to be many conversations about a new normal, I strongly recommend that we all learn to shift gears smoothly and do our best to coordinate keeping our hand in God's hand and staying on a straight road.

# Signs

When one hears the word signs, usually a visual of some kind comes into focus. If you are driving or riding in a car, you might be thinking, red, stop sign; yellow, yield sign; or perhaps a No U-Turn sign. If it is time for a season change, the visual could be snow and icy roads. Better yet, the mind might focus on beautiful blossoms, green grass, green leaves, and bright sunshine.

In an election year, we are inundated with political signs. Candidates are vying for votes by displaying their pictures and platforms on yard signs, billboards, and newspaper ads. All signs of an upcoming voting day and political competitions.

Other signs that certainly need our attention are things like shortness of breath or chest pains. These signs require medical attention and possibly are warnings of imminent danger.

Remembering and utilizing the acronym FAST will help you quickly recognize the signs of a stroke.

- Face: Check the smile. Does one side of his or her face droop?
- Arms: When attempting to raise both arms, does one arm drift downward?
- Speech: When trying to repeat a simple phrase, is speech slurred or strange?
- Time: If any of these signs are clearly visible, know that time is crucial and the important thing to do is dial 911 immediately!

Finding a lump in your breast or noticing other unnatural body changes are other sure signs that one should seek medical attention. Know your body and pay close attention to changes—remember, signs are there to help protect us. They are for our benefit and we must learn not to ignore them. Whether it is a Stop sign, change of season sign, health warning—pay attention and take heed!

The one sign that so many, myself included, try to ignore, and unfortunately treat with little respect is PAIN. Pain has been referred to as "the gift nobody wants." Think about that. Pain—a gift? When you really think about it, pain is a precious gift. It forces you to concentrate on a problem area and hopefully respond to it. Without pain our lives would be open to abuse and horrible decay. Thank God for pain. While pain is unpleasant, it is the force that will cause us, for example, to withdraw our fingers from a hot stove. That very quality saves us from destruction. The point being, unless the warning signals demand response, we might not heed it. If you break a bone and are taking aspirins or painkillers to dull the throbbing, it is hard to be grateful for pain. But think about it, that pain is alerting the body to danger and hopefully preventing you from compounding the injury.

C. S. Lewis used the phrase, "Pain, the megaphone of God." Pain is truly a shout that something is wrong. Therefore, while we do not relish the idea of being in pain, or look forward to pain, hopefully we can come to the realization that, pain is a gift.

The "Footprints" poem reminds us that through the pain, or whatever—God will never leave us or forsake us. I believe God sometimes uses pain to tell us to trust Him.

Signs warn us, protect us, and often save us from harm or danger. Heed all signs!

"He rescues and He saves; He performs signs and wonders in the heavens and on the earth..." (Daniel 6:27).

# Small Change: Fantastic Results

*T*here is a theory that if you do something consecutively for thirty days, it will become a habit. Some say, it takes less time. It all depends on the person and the anticipated expectation.

It could be something as simple as walking around the block every morning. If you do this, it could improve your circulation, strengthen muscles, and even take off some excess weight. The benefits of this small change in your daily routine could prove nearly miraculous.

Change one word in your vocabulary and you will see a change in your whole attitude. Start replacing the word "have" with the word "get." Sound strange? Try it.

Think about all the times you say, "I have to go…" Change that to "I get to go…" Aren't you thankful that you are able to go wherever and do whatever?

"I must do laundry" becomes "I get to do laundry." Thank God that you have soap powder, clothes, sheets, etc., to wash. Many are not as fortunate.

Change "I must pay bills" to "I get to pay bills." That means you can afford to have utilities, a home, a car and possibly some credit cards. What a blessing to have funds available to take care of your needs!

"I get to wash dishes because I have running water!" How many areas in the world—and some not so distant—do not have the luxury of clean, running water at their disposal? You are blessed!

"I get to take my car for repairs because I have one." Wow!

"I get to go shopping for groceries." Have you ever witnessed people searching through garbage cans behind restaurants or seen pictures of families and children plowing through garbage for left-over scraps of food? Shopping for groceries becomes a gratifying experience.

"I get to prepare dinner for my family, because I have food, a family and am not alone." If cooking was a chore, it now becomes a privilege and an opportunity to serve.

"I get to mow the lawn, rake leaves, trim bushes, and prune trees, because I have a yard." "Praise the Lord your God for the good land he has given you" (Deuteronomy 8:10).

These are just a few of the things you get to do purely by the grace of God.

There is so much to be thankful for when you look at life with an attitude of gratitude!

When you make a small change in your daily vocabulary, it is the beginning of seeing fantastic results in your life and spiritual walk. Counting your blessings may have started as a routine to help rock you to sleep at night, but living those blessings daily make you realize that, "Blessed are those who trust in the LORD and have made the LORD their hope and confidence" (Jeremiah 17:7).

Counting your blessings can result in a permanent fantastic attitude adjustment!

# Small, Short Steps

*A*s we usher in March, let's reflect on February—the short-est month of our calendar year. Fleeting thoughts embrace Black History Month and the celebration or lack thereof, of the celebration of the significance of African American contributions throughout American history.

The designation of February as Black History month had a tur-tle like beginning. It wasn't until Carter G. Woodson, plagued by the misrepresentation and underrepresentation of African Americans in American history took a seemingly small step toward reshaping the study of American history. In 1915, along with Jesse E. Moorland, he founded the Association for the Study of Negro, or the ASALH. This organization would promote studying Black history as a discipline and celebrate the accomplishments of African Americans. Then in February 1926, Woodson and the ASALH launched a "Negro History Week." Initially they chose the second week in February because it encompassed both Frederick Douglass's birthday on February 14 and Abraham Lincoln's birthday on February 12. That blows my theory on why February! Explanation to follow.

As celebrations and studies spread, understanding became more prevalent. The Civil Rights movement in the 1960s is evidence that Black history could and would no longer be completely ignored. Eventually, mayors across the country adopted "Negro History Week," and in 1976, President Gerald Ford decreed Black History Month a national observance.

The sweat and tears endured and the service that African Americans provided was swept under the carpet for years/centuries. Our country seemingly saw African American presence and contributions as indifferent, and this led to blatant insensitivity. It seems that any contributions were insignificant and once the slaves were free, we/they became invisible. What a sad state!

For those that do care, we owe the celebration of Black History Month to Carter G. Woodson, and we acknowledge him as the father of Black history. Carter G. Woodson is a hero. He worked his way from the coalmines in Kentucky, son of former slaves, to become a Harvard-educated historian and journalist. His passion to help other become aware of the true history of our country led him to seek changes in the education and understanding of African American contributions to our society. He started where he was, with what he had. This is an incentive for each of us to do the same!

In addition to being Black History Month, February is also designated as Heart Awareness Month. Many advertisements and promotions display reminders to take care of your heart, eat right, exercise regularly, and to keep a regular check on that essential organ in your body. Then with Valentine's Day in the middle of this month, there is cupid and the Love theme. Sermons emphasize love and relationships. Florists make a bundle on folks sending flowers and other tokens of love to their loved ones. Chocolate sales soar as heart shaped boxes of those sweet things are delivered. All in the name of love!

Thinking about Healthy Heart awareness (you can't live without a heart) and Valentine's Day (we all need love) is it not a reasonable thought that God planted and grew the seed for Black History month to coincide with these two celebrations? It has been said that "Providence is the intersection of God's sovereignty and God's goodness. Providence is God's work in the seemingly coincidental events in our lives." It can all be summed up in John 13:34: "A new command I give you; Love one another. As I have loved you, so you must love one another."

So in line with the celebration of notable historical contributions, put first things first—learn to love one another.

# Snip, Snip, Cut...

*I* have a passion for indoor green plants and provide a home for probably more than my fair share. Plants are in almost every room of my home, but there is one area that is fondly (I think) referred to as Aunt Jo's jungle. This hobby, pastime, whatever, can be time consuming and periodically requires manicuring. This means that it is often necessary to do some snipping, cutting trimming, repotting, transplanting, and thinning out, etc. Leaves may need to be removed. Stems and dying blossoms may need trimmed, and oft times small branches must even be cut off. In addition to watering the plants, there are times when they need plant food and leaf shine and maybe even new soil. All this manicuring is to keep the plants, green, healthy, blossoming, and continuing to grow and thrive. The benefits are great. The plants provide moisture to the air in the home and make an esthetic, calming atmosphere. In addition, my plants do not talk back. They do not miss curfew and I always know where they are.

When taking care of the plants, I often think about the scripture, "I am the vine, and my Father is the gardener. He cuts off every branch in me that bears no fruit, while every branch that does bear fruit, he prunes so that it will be even more fruitful."

This thinking takes me to the various branches in your life and mine. Is pruning not a wise way to handle and care for the relationships, habits, service, and every day "things" in all our lives? Do we need to seriously consider trimming personal branches? What areas in our life do we need to snip, snip, and cut? Cut habits that are keeping us from leading a wholesome life, and consider replacements such as love deeply, laugh heartily, and pray daily. Plan for more daily nourishment—like a good Bible study and/or more quality time with family and "good" friends. As you begin to tend to the branches in your life, remember, "Only what you do for Christ will last."

Since we all know what assume means. I will not assume that you will consider "pruning" as a way to take care of yourself and your life, but I will encourage you to regularly check your branches and evaluate how healthy they are and what care they may need. Personally, I thank God for the beautiful greenery in my life and the pleasure it brings. That thankfulness includes the facts that the plants do not need a daily walk, they make no noise, and the only cleanup is a few falling leaves. So with my plants as a starting point, I am on a journey to snip, snip and cut!

"She considers a field and buys it; out of her earnings she plants a vineyard" (Proverbs 31:16).

# Some Whys of Life

Why do we so often sit and wonder "why"? That little three-letter word is almost as conflicting as "if." It makes us think, why did this happen? Why did she say that?

Why did they do that? Why didn't I get the job? Why am I fat? Why can't I lose weight? Why aren't my prayers being answered? Why, why, why?

Why does the past glide away so easily and the present drift, and sometimes they collide?

Why—all at once the mornings are slow, eyesight gets blurry, and memory becomes brittle?

Why are the once certainties now questionable—like the day of the week, tying of a shoelace, rhythm of a prayer, directions to a favorite place? Why?

Why is there a slippage of memory?

Why am I feeling blue and lonely?

Why am I not doing more with my life? Why am I not able to do more or have the energy I once had?

Many of the whys is the result of maturing/aging! So instead of being consumed with the whys, let us refocus and adjust our thinking as follows:

I would never trade my amazing friends, my wonderful life, or my loving family for a flatter belly or less gray hair.

I will not chide myself for eating that extra cookie (gaining a little weight), or not making my bed, or for buying that figurine that I did not need. I am entitled to a treat, to be a little messy, or to be somewhat extravagant. I have seen too many dear friends leave this world too soon; before they had the opportunity to enjoy or understand the great freedom that comes with aging.

Whose business is it if I choose to read, watch TV, or play games on the computer until 4:00 AM and sleep until noon? I can even dance with myself to the wonderful tunes of the sixties and seventies and reminisce about those good old days, and perhaps weep over a lost love…

Feeling blue or lonely is normal, when you remember the loved ones that are gone, when you see a child suffering, or someone loses a beloved pet. These feelings can strengthen you, give you deeper understanding, and equip you to be able to show compassion for others.

As you get older, it is easier to be positive. You worry less about what others think and you question yourself less. Aging is almost like being Saved—you are set free! You know that you are not going to live forever, so do not waste time lamenting over the whys, what could have been, or worrying about what will be. Be busy about doing God's will. Go and "bear fruit—fruit that will last."

It is never too late to become the person you can become. Wear yourself out doing good, helping others, and being a blessing to someone. Do not just sit around and accumulate rust! Know that "only what you do for Christ will last."

"He gives strength to the weary and increases the power of the weak. Even youths grow weary, and young men stumble and fall; But those who hope in the Lord will renew their strength. They will soar on wings like eagles; they will run and not grow weary, and they will walk and not be faint" (Isaiah 40:29–31).

Push the whys aside—live heartily, love deeply, and pray daily!

# Stop! Look! Listen! Obey!

$\mathcal{S}$ top, look, listen, and obey. These words could very easily apply to driving a vehicle, and the traffic signals and signs that are in place for our protection. They could also be applicable to life and the situations and conditions that surround us.

Have you ever seriously pondered your surrounding environment and analyzed how that environment influences and forms your entire being? Stop, look, listen, and obey!

Pastor preached a dynamic sermon, as usual, this past Sunday, and upon reviewing my notes many different scenarios floated through my mind. In addition, a column in the newspaper about the clean, wholesome lyrics penned by Brad Paisley confirmed my direction.

God said, "Let there be light..." and just by speaking, in a moment, the environment changed. Unfortunately, we do not always have the power to immediately change our environments, but when we have that choice, stop, look at the options, listen to what God is telling you, and obey.

Your home environment could be either life or death to you and those within. When the household/home is filled with nurturing love and compassion, more than likely a healthy, positive person will emerge. On the other hand, if there is constant bickering, fighting, cursing, and abuse, a "bully" might be the outcome. The home environment sets the stage for one's life journey!

Depending on the dynamics, the management, and co-workers, the workplace environment can cause one to succeed or fail. Think about the boss from "hell"! Hopefully, he/she went back there and got off your back. But just in case they are still around, take time to stop (pray), look (for another job), listen (for all opportunities available), and obey (get moving)!

Watching TV is an environment under your control. What are you watching? Is it something that uplifts and helps you develop mentally and spiritually? If not, think seriously about making some changes. Remember, you can control that dial!

What do you listen to in the car? Here you have many choices. Whether it is a radio station, CDs, or tapes, make wise choices. Choose uplifting sounds that will keep you calm while you are driving and give you peace and joy. As mentioned above, Brad Paisley is a great "clean" choice! Another positive choice is Byron Cage—especially his song, "The Presence of the Lord is Here."

With whom do you spend your time? Are they positive individuals? Is the relationship a healthy one? Do you mutually respect each other? Stay away from "Debbie Downer." Stop, look, and listen at your relationships. Whom do you call "friend"? Friends range from casual acquaintances to those who would die for you. Sometimes friends are closer than brothers or sisters. Friends share affection, companionship, confidences, consideration, devotion, helpfulness, loyalty, support, sympathy, trust, and understanding. This choice of "environment" is a HUGE factor in your life! Make sure you handle it with prayer!

Know that your environment is critical. While we are always in His presence, make sure we are engaged with His presence!

Stop: "Be still, and know that I am God..." (Psalms 46:10).

Look: "I sought the LORD, and He answered me: He delivered me from all my fears" (Psalms 34:4–5).

Listen: "Listen to His voice and hold fast to Him" (Deuteronomy 30:20).

Obey: "This is love for God to obey His commands..." (1 John 5:3).

# Superglue

*I*f you have ever used superglue you know its strength. Superglue is wonderful for fixing broken items. It allows you to reattach that handle to an heirloom teacup, the arm to the antique doll, the gem on your favorite bracelet and many other things are often made useable and beautiful again, using superglue.

But you must be very careful that you do not get superglue on your fingers. While it is great for putting things back together, it can be extremely harmful and damaging if it gets on your skin.

If you are facing a tough situation, going through painful circumstances, or in the valley of despair, faithfully call on God. Think of Him as your Superglue and let Him put things back in place for you. Believe me; He can fix things better than superglue: and you don't have to be concerned about Him pulling the skin off your fingers!

If you feel like your life is falling apart, pray to God. "He is before all things, and in Him all things hold together" (Colossians 1:17).

I will share a poem that touches on this journey we are all traveling. It is entitled "Life Is...," and the author is anonymous. It goes like this:

> Life is a mystery—unfold it.
> Life is a struggle—face it.
> Life is beauty—praise it.
> Life is a puzzle—solve.
> Life is opportunity—take it.
> Life is sorrowful—experience it.

Life is a song—sing it.
Life is a mission—fulfill it.

As true as this might be, we are unable to accomplish these things on our own.

Stevie Wonder had a hit record a few years ago—"Signed, Sealed, and Delivered." I think that is a perfect way to look at the Bible and the scriptures. Parts of the lyrics to that song are "Like a fool, I went and stayed away too long..., Now I'm back and not ashamed to cry, here I am signed, sealed and delivered. You got my future in your hands... I have done a lot of foolish things that I really didn't mean... But here I am, signed, sealed, and delivered."

Just as the scriptures have been signed, sealed, and delivered to us, we need to reciprocate, and say, "Here I am Lord, all yours, signed, sealed, and delivered!"

Jesus can and will be your personal tube of superglue. He can put all things back together for you. When he fixes things, they are just like new. Call on Him and let Him infuse you with peace and strength to overcome whatever obstacles or storms you are facing. He can help you put things back together and hold them in place, as you boldly and proudly exclaim, "I can do all things through Christ which strengthens me" (Philippians 4:19). Let Jesus be your Superglue!

# Thankful and Proud

*C*ongratulations to all graduates. Whether it is high school, undergraduate (bachelor's degree), graduate (master's degree), or doctorate, you deserve a big hug and pat on the back for your hard work, perseverance, stick-to-it-ness and a job well done. Education is so much like climbing stairs. We take one step at a time to get to the top. Once you reach that top step, you still must make choices, and keep going. Learning should never stop.

To all the parents of these great kids, you are to be commended for your tenacity, encouragement, and the support you have provided over the years. We must constantly remind these young people that each step they take moves them closer and closer to their dream. Let them know that you respect them for their achievements. Also, remind them that it was God's grace that got them there. Use all the adjectives you can think of to show them that you are proud of not only what they have accomplished, but also where they are going. Do not be shy about telling them that they are special, intelligent, strong, clever, gifted, and talented and that you are so proud of them. Proverbs 22:6 tells us, "Train a child in the way he should go, and when he is old, he will not turn from it." In addition, Proverbs 22:12 tell us, "The eyes of the Lord keep watch over knowledge…" Therefore, I would say that we are the parents that realized early on, that our child was a gift from God, given and entrusted to us to raise as the scriptures admonishes us to do. Be proud of your accomplishments and theirs also.

The news is always full of the negative acts of our young people, and when the negative activity occurs, there is news coverage on every channel and in the paper for days. While graduations and graduates get a mere mention, it seems that the media thrives more on the sensational and heartbreaking incidents rather than on the positive happenings. Let us strive to pay more attention to the good!

May 10, 2014, was such a blessed day for our family as we gathered to witness my daughter march at WVU's commencement and receive her doctorate in Education. The old African proverb that states, "It takes a village to raise a child" was manifested. Truly, it was a proud moment for me and our family and friends that have stood by us over the years. However, while being proud, the stronger emotion was "thankfulness." I am constantly amazed at how God places special people in our lives, just when we need them, to get over whatever hurdles may be there, or to encourage and strengthen us when we start growing weary. He is truly an awesome God.

While being a sincerely proud and thankful Mama, there was still the need to stress to my daughter that no matter how many degrees she may earn, she will never be smarter than Phyllis or me. "Who is a wise man and endued with knowledge among you? Let him show out of a good conversation his works with meekness of wisdom" (James 3:13).

# Thanksgiving

*We* recently celebrated "Thanksgiving" often called "Turkey Day." This is a much-anticipated holiday with families and friends gathering to enjoy traditional family foods and often even trying new recipes. Many travel miles to join with others to share a meal that has been a labor of love! This is a favorite holiday for many, because unlike Christmas, there are no real gift expectations, and there are no real shopping frenzies—except for food!

Social service organizations and many churches do a great job providing meals to the hungry. There is often a public appeal for donations of "traditional" foods, allowing many of us to contribute, to prepare large quantities of food to feed the homeless or less fortunate folks. Kind-hearted volunteers spend many hours gathering and preparing food for the mass feedings. In addition, many other volunteers spend Thanksgiving Day serving the meals. We are all thankful for the opportunity to serve on Thanksgiving. We are thankful that we are physically, mentally, and financially able to be a part of the Thanksgiving experience.

The question is why do we just do this on the Thanksgiving Day holiday? Why does it have to be a designated Holiday for us to join forces to want to bless others and make something wonderful happen? Are people and families only hungry for a decent meal on Thanksgiving Day?

As volunteers, are we seeking comfort or inner peace by offering our service on this one day a year? Does it make us happy to be able to say, "I helped serve dinner for the homeless on Thanksgiving?" Remember, there are 364 more days in the year!

What I am trying to say is that we can get so fixated on things that really don't matter in the grand scheme of things. If we are concentrating on doing good only one day a year, are we allowing our hearts to be soft enough to really be helpful and useful throughout the rest of the year?

There is an old saying that money will buy everything but real happiness. Over time, we might want to consider what is our happy. While my pockets are full, is my heart empty? Think on this!

Give a new meaning to Thanksgiving! Do not forget about the food and feeding the hungry but add to that. Make a hard copy **gratitude** list. *(You might even consider using a pen and paper!)* Thank Jesus for what He has taught you in the midst of any struggles and for what He has brought you through. Cherish this list and move forward sharing your joy! Now we can have Thanksgiving every day!

# The Aftertaste

*M*any say that artificial sweeteners, the stuff in the yellow, pink, or blue packets, leave a distinct unpleasant aftertaste. Some say the same of diet Coke. The aftertaste is the primary reason for not using these products, and for preferring the "real stuff"—sugar. Even if a sugar-free diet is warranted and recommended, the aftertaste is prioritized. The aftertaste is remembered.

Those who have high blood pressure are often steered toward no salt or a salt substitute. Once again, the aftertaste is a problem!

The thought of avoiding small things with such a firm stance leads to thoughts of things that leave an "aftertaste" to more than your tongue and palate. What about the aftertaste caused by lust—adultery or fornication? Then there is the effect and consequences of the misuse or abuse of opioid meds, alcohol, or other drugs. Pornography must also leave a bitter aftertaste. Sin comes with an aftertaste. There may be pleasure for a minute or a season—but then, the aftertaste follows. This aftertaste can be long lasting!

We are going through a season that is unfortunately leaving a strong bitter aftertaste in society in general. The state of our nation currently has a pungent odor and taste affecting not just our taste buds but also all our senses. The history of injustice, senseless murders, racial bigotry, insensitivity, unwarranted hatred, and just plain meanness permeates and pollutes the air. COVID-19 and social unrest are ravaging in the fore front and the aftertaste is strong! It is difficult to breathe normally. The aftertaste of these pandemics is not just unpleasant, it is choking. This kind of aftertaste smothers any previous progress and leaves a permanent stain on many lives.

To avoid the aftertaste of artificial sweeteners, we could try using honey. That is a potential solution. If salt substitutes are so unacceptable, one might try vinegar, lemon juice or some herbs. That would circumvent that aftertaste.

To forgo the problems, concerns, and aftertaste in this season of pandemics, let's start with Psalm 51:10, "Create in me a clean heart, O God; and renew a right spirit within me." We all know we must begin someplace, so let it begin with me and you. "The Sovereign LORD is my strength! He will make me as surefooted as a deer and bring me safely over the mountains" (Habakkuk 3:19).

There is a way to eliminate the aftertaste! Believe and trust in JESUS! Follow His teachings and be obedient to the Word.

# The Ds

*A* D is not a good grade. During the school years, a D shows that you are close to failing. A D in some courses also meant that you had to take that class over again—especially if it was in your major, or a required course. Ds could also delay promotion to the next grade or even graduation.

In business, a D rating is a strong indication that you probably should not do business with that company. It is a warning for consumers.

In business and in school, most people strive for the A. An A indicates that you have learned something—that you are proficient in each area or task. You have gained and shown proof of your knowledge. For a business to receive an A rating, it tells one that the business is reputable. They provide excellent customer service. They have fair pricing. They have qualified employees…

In our daily lives, there are some D words that also spell trouble and failings in our walk. A few of the D words are as follows:

**Disobedience**: The refusal to obey. There are rules, spoken and sometimes unspoken, that we should follow. It could be as simple as stopping at the STOP signs. Rules are for our protection or to protect someone else. Think about what could happen if you ignored STOP signs. The result could be fines from the traffic violation or even worse, an accident or a fatality. There are many scriptures related to obedience and disobedience. One found in Proverbs 19:16 tell us this, "He who obeys instructions guards his life, but he who is contemptuous of his ways will die." To strive for the A, we must have an attitude adjustment and learn to practice obedience.

**Doubt**: To be undecided or skeptical or to disbelieve. Doubting is lack of confidence in you, others, and in our Savior. We must have faith and learn to believe and trust in the truths in the Bible. "He who doubts is like a wave of the sea, blown and tossed by the wind. That man should not think he will receive anything from the Lord; he is a double-minded man, unstable in all he does" (James 1:6–7). Accepting the truth is the first step toward our good grade of A.

**Denial**: Refusal to accept the truth, rejection of reality. We cannot fix or even begin to work on a problem until we admit that it is a problem. Acknowledging and Accepting the truth is the first step toward our good grade of A. Know that there is work to do and do it. Do not let this D word block your blessings. "If you harbor bitter envy and self-ambition in your hearts, do not boast it or deny the truth" (James 3:14).

**Disregard**: To treat without proper respect or attention. Every day we read news articles about abuse, neglect, and lack of respect for someone's property or life. Every newscast reveals much of the same. People seem to have no respect for others. What used to be an exchange of words, or at worst, a fistfight, now is a shooting or stabbing. What has happened to our society? We do not even respect or seem to place value on our bodies. We do not take care of ourselves or those that are entrusted to our care. The A here is to strive to be Accountable for all that we say or do. "I want men everywhere to lift up holy hands in prayer, without anger or disputing" (1 Timothy 2:9).

With these D words invading our lives, we need to announce loudly and clearly, "Not today Satan, and tomorrow neither." Anchor your soul and your life in His Word. Build a solid foundation through prayer and studying His word and your anchor will hold. Hang on to the As. Leave the Ds in the sea of forgetfulness.

# The Gift Nobody Wants

*W*e have just passed through the "season of giving"— Christmas. A time when most folks generously give, share, and go the full gamut of being an example of love. Oft times gifts are given just for the sake of giving and not much thought is put into how, or even if the gift will be used. Too many times, I believe some of the gifts are "recycled"! This can be dangerous because that same gift just might be returned to the original giver. This is when you discover, it's a gift no one wants. Some gifts are exchanged, and the receiver can get something he or she really wants. Other gifts may just sit around collecting dust. Then there are some gifts that are just trashed—a gift nobody wants!

While recovering from an extended hospital stay, I revisited some old reading materials. Among them was a pamphlet entitled "The gift nobody wants." How interesting!

This pamphlet, written by Philip Yancey, precisely described my recent struggles. I have been dealing with back issues and sciatic pain for what seems like much too long. So when severe, excruciating, continuous pain racked this body, I was beginning to believe that undoubtedly the progression of spine issues was making back surgery inevitable.

A much-dreaded trip to the emergency room revealed a shocking diagnosis about this recent pain. While some of the pain was from previously diagnosed problems, this new tear-jerking, constant pain was from blood clots throughout my body. The massive clotting throughout was attempting to cut off circulation to my legs and lower torso. This pain, I pray I will never experience again, was truly a gift I did not want. But the gift saved my life, sending me to the ER just in time. I had become accustomed to "if I lie down and elevate my legs, and rest, the pain will subside." And it would—for a few minutes. But then, this pain—a gift I did not want—reached a point when nothing could/would give relief.

The body was screaming for help, trying to let me know that something was definitely wrong and the pain was like a megaphone echoing in my ears and throughout my body. The pain demanded attention.

Once given the diagnosis, and the prognosis, all fear and anxiety subsided. Lying there in the hospital, the gospel song "God Specializes" came to mind and the lyrics kept running through my mind giving me a peace I cannot explain.

The following scriptures were also a confirmation that I was in "GOOD" hands:

> "You will keep in perfect peace him whose minds are steadfast, because they trust in you." (Isaiah 26:3)
> "I will lie down in peace and sleep, for you alone, O LORD, will keep me safe." (Psalm 4:8)
> "Yes, my soul finds rest in God; my hope comes from him." (Psalm 62:5)

After much prayer, three surgical procedures, performed by fantastic, caring compassionate doctors at Ruby, a short stay at Health South, I am well on the way to a complete healing.

I stand steadfast in proclaiming that my God is a good God, even though He gave me a gift I did not want! (pain).

"God specializes and He can do what no other power can do!"

# The Householder

While browsing through some old files, I came across a company newsletter that I had saved from about twenty years ago. The following story is well worth sharing.

Once upon a time, a householder lived with his wife, his two small children, and his elderly parents in a very small hut.

The man did his best to be helpful and patient, but the house and the crowding in the hut suddenly became too much. His parents coughed and made demands. His wife scolded. In addition, the children cried.

One day, in utter desperation, the householder went to the village's wise man to ask what he should do to ease the overcrowding and the noise.

"Do you have a rooster?" asked the wise man.

"Yes," replied the householder.

"Then, put the rooster inside your hut, too, and come back to see me in a week."

A week later, the householder returned and told the wise man that his situation was now even more desperate. The rooster crowed morning and night and made the hut a mess.

"Do you have a cow?" asked the wise man.

"Yes," replied the householder.

"Then, put that cow inside your hut, too, and come back to see me in a week."

A week later, the man returned, and in the next three weeks, despite his increasing complaints, he followed the wise man's orders and took into his home his brother's children, a goat, and his chickens.

Finally, the householder could stand it no longer. He ran to the wise man and screamed, "I can't bear this anymore. I came to you for a solution. Now there is absolutely no room in my hut, and there's not a moment's quiet."

"Okay," said the wise man. "Now put everything out of your house except your wife, your two children, and your parents.

And he did. Without the rooster, the cow, the brother's children, the goat, and the chickens, the house suddenly became very spacious, very clean, and very quiet—and everyone lived happily ever after.

Moral of the story: Sometimes we do not know how well off we really are.

This story is quite similar to the parable about the prodigal son. Read Luke 15:11–32 and see if you see the similarity!

# The Right Key

*I*f you were to look up the word key in the dictionary, some of the definitions you would find are as follows: a metal notched and grooved instrument that is turned to open a lock; something that is a means of access, control, or possession; a vital, crucial element; a set of answers to a test; the keystone in the crown of an arch; a button or lever that is pressed with the finger to operate a machine; a button or lever that is pressed with the finger to produce or modulate the sound of a musical instrument, as in a clarinet or piano; the pitch of a voice or other sound; a kilogram of marijuana or heroin; a low offshore island; and the definitions continue.

Recently we had the door locks to our home changed. My daughter kept the keys for the old locks in her purse and inadvertently misplaced the new keys. Consequently, she had to ring the doorbell to gain access. She did not have the right key.

Most of us have several keys in our possession. We have door keys. We have keys to our home safe. We might have a key for a diary or journal. We have car keys, or at least a device for that keyless ignition starter. Some may even have keys to a bank safe deposit box. Many may have a mailbox key. All these keys serve a purpose, but each key is designed to open a particular lock. If you do not have the right key, you will not be able to gain access. Several years ago, before TSA, it was important to have a good lock and key for your suitcase or luggage. Many folks have been presented with an honorary "key to the city." Unfortunately, this key, while complimentary and sometimes beautiful, is a faux pas. It does not open anything!

All the above keys are tangible items and command the right fit for successful access.

There is another key-the most important key—a personal relationship with Jesus. This is the key that unlocks the door to God's presence and to our prayers. This key does not require special curves, grooves, or tones. This key commands acceptance and faith.

> "What other nation is so great as to have their gods near them the way the Lord our God is near us whenever we pray to him?" (Deuteronomy 4:6)
> "You may ask anything in my name, and I will do it." (John 14:6)

A personal relationship with Jesus, it is the only key you need. That is the right key to salvation. Stay faithful and use it. It is your right and privilege as the Father's child.

# The Terrible Ts

*Y*ou often hear folks talk about the terrible twos, referring to that period when a toddler turns two years of age. For some, it seems that this is a very challenging time. The toddler is very ambulatory and quick on their feet, and with their hands. Anything within reach is fair game for their little mouths, and sometimes for their ears. My nephew recently had to visit urgent care because his little darling wanted to see what it felt like to put playdough in her ears. Parents share many stories about how they patiently and thankfully survived this stage of life. Although you hear many negative stories, the terrible twos have many rewarding teachable moments that we need to anticipate and be prepared to take advantage of in a positive manner.

The terrible twos are mild in comparison to the Ts that invade our lives on this journey through life—that would be troubles, trials, and temptations. It is almost like comparing Heinz Ketchup to Texas Pete Hot Sauce. Regardless of age, gender, race, or economic status, there are times when one, or all those Ts confront us full force and linger for a while. How do you overcome and survive? Faith!

Years ago, I heard a sermon, "This is just a test." This pastor advised that we should consider trials, temptations, and troubles as a test of our faithfulness. If we could just learn to seek His face and acknowledge His presence, He will provide the strength and direction we need to make it through which ever T faces us. "I can do everything through him who gives me strength" (Philippians 4:13).

He provides all the tools that we need. Not only will He provide us with the tools, but He will also direct our paths. Our part is to seek His face and listen.

Alexander McLaren said, "Each of us may be sure that if God sends us on stony paths, He will provide us with strong shoes."

Don't ever try to be a martyr and think you alone are strong enough to handle the terrible Ts on your own—in private—use your wisdom and faith, cast all your cares and burdens on one who knows exactly what to do with them and how to handle each and every one. "My grace is sufficient for you, for my power is made perfect in weakness" (2 Corinthians 12:9).

"He performs wonders that cannot be fathomed, miracles that cannot be counted" (Job 5:9).

The terrible Ts do not destroy your joy and peace. Live in His will, guided and protected to be blessed, so that you can be a blessing. The terrible Ts are just a test.

# The True Color of Friendships

riendship is the relationship of mutual affection between people. Some might want a more specific definition and clarification such as mutual friend, close friend, childhood friend, real friend, or perhaps Facebook friend. Each one has its own special meaning.

Someone once said, "Show me your friends, and you'll show me your future." This statement has a lot of merit and draws on biblical wisdom. Ponder this...

Growing up, there were probably some children either in school or in the neighborhood that your parents did not want you to associate with. And once you entered those teen years, there was probably even more scrutiny on your associates. The reasons varied from, they are too much older than you, they use profanity, they do not belong to or attend any church, and they dress too provocatively, and so on...

Once you reached the age where you made decisions about friend choices, you realized that friends come in a variety of shapes, sizes, and even categories. There are traveling friends—someone who not only enjoys traveling with you but also can afford to do so. There are shopping friends—someone who likes to hunt for bargains or just browse the stores looking at the latest styles. Then there is the confidant—the one who shares your secrets, knows your strengths and weaknesses, and loves you anyway! Then many of have virtual friends—Facebook friends—followers on Instagram and Twitter.

It is a wonderful thing if you can find several or all these attributes in one person, but that is highly unlikely.

Considering that friendship is a mutual affection, how do we account for so little love and so much loneliness when there are such a variety of friendships? Think about the type and basis for your so-called friendships. Where is the love? The mutual connection?

Proverbs 17:17 tells us, "A friend loves at all times..."

Proverbs 18:24 cautions us, "A man of many companions may come to ruin, but there is a friend who sticks closer than a brother." Is your friend available to help you weather the storms in your life, or are they just available for the good times?

Think about the drug and opioid problems in our society today. People are becoming addicted because a "friend" shared with them. What a friend! Again, where is the love?

People are committing all kind of heinous acts of violence and torture and sharing with their Facebook friends. Is this affection?

"Anyone who chooses to be a friend of the world becomes an enemy of God." (James 4:4)

"Walk with the wise and become wise, for a companion of fools suffers harm." (Proverbs 13:20)

"The godly give good advice to their friends, the wicked lead them astray." (Proverbs 12:26)

So show me your friends—your real friends—and you will show me your future!

# Them and Us

*I*t is sad that there is so much separation in the world today allowing for Them and Us to be so blatantly expressed.

The stone walls of bigotry and the fences of hatred, along with misunderstanding and ignorance, establish boundaries that divide and separate, creating the Them and Us. Some of the words that clearly establish that division are as follows: Black, White; gay, straight; democrat, republican; friend, enemy; married, single; educated, uneducated; addict, clean; renter, owner, believers, nonbelievers; homeless; and disabled. All of these words serve to identify people and too often cause many of us to think negatively—them and us.

When will we realize that relationships, or the lack thereof affects all that we do and all that we are? We need to decrease, if not eliminate, the Them and Us.

While the devil builds these walls of separation, the sweet, pure, and unending love of Christ can blast through those walls, tear down the fences, and heal the wounds, if we only accept and allow His love to penetrate our stony hearts. The Them and Us will wither and fade in the brilliant light of Christ's love. Love is the key!

1 Corinthians 12 explains that every believer is a member of Christ's body and has a definite purpose. Paul uses rhetorical irony, when he poses situations such as "If the ear shall say, Because I am not the eye, I am not of the body, is it not of the body?" Paul concludes that all parts of the body are there for a reason. The body has a common bloodstream and a central nervous system. These nourish and control every part of the body. The individual parts cannot function separately. Our communities, our churches, and our surroundings are all comprised of people with differences—just like the

different parts of the body. We need each other to function well. So why so much division? Romans 8:37–39 tells us, "In all these things we are more than conquerors through Him that loved us. For I am convinced that neither death nor life, neither angels nor demons… nor anything else in all creation, will be able to separate us from the love of God that is in Christ Jesus our Lord."

We as people on this earth, all have a place and reason for being. We, who call ourselves Christians, should not have, "not my kind," in our vocabulary, or have a negative attitude of Them and Us. As Paul also reminds us in Galatians 3:28, in Him "there is neither Jew nor Greek…slave nor free…male nor female; for you are all one in Christ Jesus." This says to me that, whether others are different in attitude, race, perspective, political slant, class, or social standing, it should make no difference to those of us who call ourselves by Jesus's name.

If you know you have caused disunity or have a heart of Them and Us, sincerely pray about it, and then go find someone that is not your kind and share Jesus's love with them. I guarantee, it will make a difference in your life and theirs.

# This Is Just a Test

*H*as there been a time you were asked or ordered to do something that seemed menial or pointless? How did you respond? How did you feel? What did you do?

Do you know why you did or said what you did? Do you know why it evoked such emotion? Was there a thought lurking in the back of your mind saying, *This is absurd!* Perhaps, you decided to do the task quickly and be done. Maybe since you did not think it was important, you didn't do your best work.

Give this some thought. Were you being tested? Could it be that you were given a task to prepare you for something more?

A story passed down through the years tells of a young man meeting the head teacher for the first time. The teacher abruptly said, "The classroom needs sweeping. Take the broom and sweep it."

The young man knew this might be his only chance to impress. He swept the floor thoroughly three times. Then he dusted all the furniture four times. When the teacher returned, she used her handkerchief to inspect the room. Not finding one speck of dust, she said quietly, "I guess you will do to enter this institution."

That young man was Booker T. Washington, and the classroom was what we know today as Hampton University—an HBU (Historical Black College). That sweeping exercise was basically his entrance exam to a place of higher learning. Sharing this story in his autobiography, **Up from Slavery**, Booker T. Washington wrote this: "I have passed many examinations since then, but I have always felt this was the best one I ever passed." I wonder how many of us would have had such a humble attitude.

There is an anonymous quote that says, "If a task is once begun, never leave it till it's done. Be the labor great or small, do it well or not at all." Whatever the test, do your best!

Keep in mind, doors are opened best by a consistently excellent effort. Slacking off, goofing off, or just doing enough to get by, rarely open the doors of opportunity.

What a blessing it would be to claim these words: "I have glorified thee on earth; I have finished the work which thou gavest me to do…" (John 17:4). And then to know that you, like Booker T., passed the test, when you hear the words, "Well done, good and faithful servant. You have been faithful with a few things; I will put you in charge of many thigs. Come and share your master's happiness!" (Matthew 25:21).

Be ready for the test!

# This Is the Season

*T*his is the time of year when many are reflecting on memories of past years and the joyous times of opening Christmas presents, or hiding presents from kids, or kids finding presents that you thought were well hidden. It is also a time to reflect on how you celebrated Christmas.

Most Christians find this season very humbling and beginning the first of December make a special effort to observe this season as a spiritual preparation for Christmas—Jesus's birthday! A conscious effort may be made to pray and give thanks. Referred to as Advent Season, it is an exciting time of expectation and preparation for the celebration of the Nativity of Jesus at Christmas. Advent season officially is the period beginning four Sundays before Christmas. However, many begin their celebration December 1.

When my daughter was a year old, I spent weeks making a large Advent calendar. The background was red felt with about a twenty-four-inch green felt Christmas tree appliquéd in the center. Green sequins adorned the tree like garland. At the base of the tree, there were twenty-four pockets, with white numbers from 1–24. Inside each pocket was a beautiful, carefully made appliquéd felt ornament. The ornaments were a variety of items symbolic of Christmas—drum, candy cane, bell, candle, star, etc. Also, in each pocket, there was a scripture. The star was always in the pocket 24. Beginning December 1, we would remove the ornament from pocket 1 and place it on the tree. We would read the Bible verse, discuss it, and pray. The same ritual took place each day thereafter, building up excitement, until December 24 when the star was placed at the top of the tree. Sometime on December 24, we would make a birthday cake for the big celebration on December 25. On Christmas day, we would sing "Happy Birthday, Jesus," read from Luke 2, and enjoy the cake! Each year, the tree (Advent calendar) was carefully packed away and twenty years later, it still looked brand new. This tradition continued through elementary, middle, and high school. What precious memories!

If you have children, grandchildren, nieces of nephews Advent season is an excellent time to introduce them to the true meaning of Christmas. This is the season to take time to pray, bless others, be thankful and enjoy each day that you are blessed to see. Happy holidays!

# Three Words

*D*uring the Christmas season, many television specials seem to have a special focus on giving, sharing, or just doing good deeds. The themes primarily center on Santa Claus or Jesus, and people's beliefs on the validity of these two famous men. While wrapping Christmas gifts, my daughter and I watched several Christmas movies and specials. The two that were most thought provoking and brought the most enjoyment were the HBO movies, *Black Nativity* and *Best Man Holiday*.

*Black Nativity* brought a clear message on the devastation brought on by harboring an unforgiving spirit. This movie followed a family that was literally torn apart, separated, and isolated from each other for years, because of pride and the unwillingness to forgive one another's mistakes and bad choices. Years passed and there was no contact, no memories to share, no holidays enjoyed together, no visible love shared, and no communication. After much hardship, trying times and finally hitting "rock bottom" the family was finally reunited. The unforgiving spirit was like cancer or acid slowly destroying all the good that should have been prevalent in this family's life. So much time was lost. So many happy times were missed. However, the bittersweet conclusion showed the healing power and beauty of being accountable and forgiving. Forgiving one another opened the way for their hardened hearts to love each other again. Beautiful ending!

*Best Man Holiday* brought a group of friends and their families together for the Christmas holiday. Each one of these men had deep seated issues that were controlling their lives and keeping them from reaching their potential and doing God's will. Once again, however, it took a tragedy to get their attention and turn their lives around. During the movie, one of the men posed the following question: "If asked to describe your life in three words, what would they be?" The three words were extremely different from each man and revealed what kind of life they were living. Staring at me, my daughter asked me the same question. My immediate response was God, family, and service. However, that question was and is penetrating and thought provoking. It is something that probably needs to be digested and given more thought. How would you describe your life in three words? Give that question some serious thought and think about the "reason for all seasons." "Pleasant words are a honeycomb, sweet to the soul and healing to the bones" (Proverbs 16:24).

# Time Is a Precious Gift

*H*ow do you perceive time? How do you use this valuable resource? Do you take your time here on earth for granted?

I believe time is more valuable than money. It is one thing that is irreplaceable!

I believe my time and your time deserves equal respect and protection.

Are you one who constantly or often puts off doing something thinking, "I'll do it tomorrow?" Will there be a tomorrow for you? By procrastinating, who has been deprived of your love, your attention, your presence?

Psalms 90:12 tells us, "So teach us to number our days that we may gain hearts of wisdom."

Be grateful for each day and use your time wisely. Invest your time in people and projects that will live on after you are gone. Use your precious time to be a friend. Share your gifts, talents, and love. Know that regardless of your age, physical condition, or circumstances, you have something to contribute and you can make a difference.

There is no magic age for you to start or stop making a difference. Young, middle-aged, or mature, you can excel and make a difference in someone's life. Take some time to carefully read and absorb Ecclesiastes 3. You may get a different perspective of your gift of time and how you should use time.

Too many of us look at age-the time we have already been here on earth—and make an assumption of capabilities and value. Ponder over these statistics: Thomas Jefferson was only thirty-three when he drafted the Declaration of Independence. Benjamin Franklin was twenty-three when he wrote *Poor Richards Almanac*. Charles Dickens was twenty-four when he began the *Pickwick Papers* and twenty-five when he penned *Oliver Twist*. *Isaac Newton was twenty-four when he formulated The Law of Gravitation. Martin Luther King Jr. became one of the most visible spoke person and leader in the Civil Rights movement giving his famous "I Have a Dream" speech before being assassinated at the age of thirty-nine.* On the other end on the spectrum, Emmanuel Kant wrote his finest philosophical works at the age of seventy-four. Verdi was eighty when he produced Falstaff and eighty-five when he completed Ave Maria. At age eighty, Goethe completed Falstaff. Tennyson was eighty when he wrote *Crossing the Bar*, and Michelangelo was eighty-seven when he completed his greatest work. Biblically, look at Abraham and Sarah. Sarah was ninety and Abraham was one hundred when Isaac was conceived. Never too old or too young to make things happen or to make lasting contributions! In addition, think about this—how young was Jesus when he made that ultimate sacrifice for you and me? (John 3:16).

Know that once time is gone, you cannot retrieve it!

"You do not even know what will happen tomorrow. What is your life? You are a mist that appears for a little while and then vanishes" (James 4:14).

Yes, life is short, and time is precious. Do not allow empty days to consume your life.

Seize that valuable resource and use the "now" wisely.

"But as for me, I trust in You, O Lord; I say, "You are my God." My times are in Your hands…" (Psalms 31:15).

# Times Are Really Changing

*T*here was a time when reference to national holidays meant the traditional ten recognized federal or national holidays that symbolized a paid holiday for the average employee. If you are "old school" like me, you probably are not aware of all the "new" national holidays. Well, I am about to share some interesting information.

Recently I overheard a conversation where the topic was "National No Panties Day." I thought, *No way!* Wrong. They showed me the meme on Facebook. Then while attending a meeting the following week, we were informed that it was "National Cheer Up Someone Day."

These two comments started the wheels turning, so the Google search began.

What a surprise!

It appears that there is an entire yearly calendar with so-called monthly bona fide National Holidays. Not only are the dates and names of these holidays listed, but also there is a history and all kinds of need to know or want to know information.

The month of June lists such days as June 1, National Say Something Nice Day; June 4, National Old Maid's Day; June 5 or first Sunday, National Cancer Survivor's Day; and June 13 is national Sewing Machine Day—who would have thought it?

Some of the interesting July holidays are the following: July 1, National Postal Worker Day; July 6, National Fried Chicken Day; July 9, National Cheer Someone up Day; July 13, National French Fries Day; July 15, National Give Something Away Day; National Ice Cream Day, third Sunday; July 23, National Day of the Cowboy. There is literally a national holiday almost each day.

The month of August reveals some rather different celebratory days. August 2 is now deemed National Coloring Book Day. This could possibly be due to the growing popularity of the adult coloring books. August 6 is National Fresh Breath (Halitosis) Day. Since you now have this critical information, you have ample time to break out the breath mints!

International Cat Day is on August 8. August 17 is National I Love my feet day. This date has scads of information. It provides tips on pampering your feet and how to prevent feet complications. It also gives information on how to recycle slightly used shoes to help the needy or those less fortunate.

Moving on to August 25, we have National Kiss and Make up Day. August 28 promotes woman's equality with National Go Topless Day! Enough of that!

You might want to amuse yourself and check out the other nine months of the year and see just what other folks are celebrating. The calendar also has open dates, so folks can make suggestions/nominations—whatever. Just be careful—before you put it out there, think about Psalm 45:1 "My heart overflows with a good theme… my tongue is the pen of a ready writer."

# Today Matters

There is a very challenging and profound saying that I often heard when I was growing up, and it goes like this: "Do not put off until tomorrow what you can do today." It seemed liked this was my parent's way to prevent procrastination and for things to be done in their time frame. Little did I know, at the time, the impact those words had on me, my attitude, and about life in general.

When there is a task before me, my goal is to complete it as soon as possible. Often that means working until the "wee-wee hours." The stick-to-it-ness often drives those around me a little crazy. Admittedly, relaxing is not my strong suit. But I am working on it, and getting better at it—I think!

**But** to me, today really matters! I have lived long enough to see several family members and very close friends, here today and gone tomorrow! One was planning to host a family gathering—tomorrow. Another was planning to travel to visit family-tomorrow. One was prepared to preach to his congregation—tomorrow! Today mattered!

Today mattered to people in the scriptures. A few of those that come to mind are as follows:

- **Lot**. In Genesis 19:15, 16, the angels urged Lot to "get up, hurry, and take his wife and daughters to safety, but Lot lingered. The men came and God had to step in for the rescue.
- **Joshua**. He made it very clear in Joshua 24:14, 15, that making today matter is a daily choice. "Choose for your-selves today whom you will serve, but as for me and my house, we will serve the Lord."

- **Nehemiah** and his builders faced such strong opposition as they were trying to construct the wall around Jerusalem that they had to work through the night with a sword in one hand and a brick in the other. Every moment counted (Nehemiah 4:16–23).
- **David**. David sang, "This is the day the Lord has made; I will rejoice and be glad in it." Later he wrote: "Today, if you hear his voice, harden not your hearts." It appears that David was very aware of the significance of today.
- **Solomon.** In Ecclesiastes 3, Solomon proclaimed that we must make the most of each day. He wrote that God has made everything appropriate in its time and there is a time for everything under the sun.
- **Paul.** Today mattered to Paul as he compared life to a race (1 Corinthians 9:24–27), and how we must stay focused on the prize/goal. Our lives should be like the runners—preparing for the finish (Philippians 3:7–14).
- **Jesus.** Today matters to Jesus as He told us In the Sermon on the Mount, "Seek first the kingdom of God and His righteousness, and all these things shall be added to you. Therefore, do not worry about tomorrow, for tomorrow will worry about its own things." In other words, focus on today.

In the book *Today Matters* there is a list of twelve recommended commitments to help make our lives better. There is biblical foundation for each one.

1. Just for today, I will choose and display the right attitude (Philippians 2:3–8).
2. Just for today, I will determine and act on important priorities (Ephesians 5:15–17).
3. Just for today, I will know and follow healthy guidelines (1 Corinthians 6:19–20).
4. Just for today, I will communicate with and care for my family (1 Timothy 5:8).

5. Just for today, I will practice and develop good thinking (Proverbs 4:5–9).
6. Just for today, I will make and keep proper commitments (Philippians 3:12–14).
7. Just for today, I will earn and properly manage my finances (Ecclesiastes 5:10–20).
8. Just for today, I will deepen and live out my faith (Colossians 2:6, 7).
9. Just for today, I will initiate and invest is solid relationships (Colossians 3:12–24).
10. Just for today, I will plan for and model generosity (Proverbs 11:24–28).
11. Just for today, I will embrace and practice good values (Psalm 119:33–40).
12. Just for today, I will seek and experience improvements (1 Peter 2:1–3).

I am convinced that today matters. Are you?

Live your life being a worthy example. "Encourage one another daily…" (Hebrews 3:13).

# Tomorrow

One of my favorite Christian songs is "Tomorrow" by the Winans. The lyrics to this song should make a person stop and think about what is important about life's journey.

Have you ever put off visiting a sick friend, and when you found the time to finally make that visit, they were not here any longer?

Has your mate, child or loved one wanted to spend time with you, but you were too busy?

Has a friend needed or wanted your company, and you said, maybe tomorrow?

Have you missed the opportunity to tell someone you loved them, thinking, next time or tomorrow and you never got another chance?

It seems that people often put more value on "tomorrow" than they do "today."

If we are to live the great life that is meant for us to live, why do we save the good things for tomorrow—which we may never see?

Does the season of our life dictate how we see tomorrow? Old or young—tomorrow is not a guarantee!

Look at the following lyrics to the Winans's version of "Tomorrow" and compare that to the version of "Tomorrow" from the movie *Annie*.

BEBE Winans's Lyrics

Jesus said, "Here I stand, won't you please let me in?"
And you said, "I will tomorrow"
Jesus said, I am He who supplies all your needs"

And you said, "I know, but tomorrow, ooh, tomorrow, I'll give my
life tomorrow, I thought about today, but it's so much easier to say"
Tomorrow, who promised you tomorrow,
Better choose the Lord today, for tomorrow
very well might be too late.
And who said tomorrow would ever come for you
Still you laugh and play and continue to say
"tomorrow"
Forget about tomorrow will not you give your life today
Please do not just turn and walk away
Tomorrow, tomorrow is not promised
Don't let this moment slip away
Your tomorrow could very well begin today.

*Annie*
Tomorrow
The sun'll come out tomorrow
Bet your bottom dollar
That tomorrow There'll be sun!
Just thinkin' about Tomorrow
Clears away the cobwebs,
And the sorrow
"Til there's none!
When I'm stuck in a day
That's gray,
And lonely,
I just stick out my chin
And grin, And say, Oh
The sun'll come out tomorrow
So ya gotta hang on
"Til' tomorrow
Come what may
Tomorrow!
Tomorrow!
I love ya tomorrow!
You are always a day away!

The Annie lyrics give a childlike, happy view of tomorrow. This is great if there is tomorrow.

The cliché "Don't put off until tomorrow what you can do today" has merit!

Proverbs 27:1 says, "Do not boast about tomorrow, for you do not know what a day may bring forth." Think on that!

Live with an open mind and heart. Know that encounters with others are gifts we give each other. Live for today—not tomorrow—to make a difference. Look for opportunities to contribute to the community, your friends, and your family by sharing your gifts and talents. Know that when you "freely" give, it will make a difference **today**, as well as tomorrow.

Material gifts are wonderful, but the greatest gifts do not fit in a box or a gift bag. They touch the heart. These gifts include kindness, joy, compassion, and love. You will find that as you open your heart and give, you will receive from others the gifts of love, wisdom, and experience. A win-win situation!

Do not waste today putting off things until tomorrow. Tomorrow is a day we may never see!

# Trees, Bushes, and Leaves

*T*his past week one of my devotional readings did a brief comparison of a flourishing "river tree" and a "shriveling bush." The location of the tree gave it every advantage to thrive, grow, and even be useful, providing shade as needed. The tree totally relied on "nature" for all its needs. And all its needs were provided. The bush or shrub was in the desert and did not have the benefit of the river, nor the good soil. Consequently, it succumbed.

As the week progressed, pictures of trees, bushes, and even leaves seemed constantly in view. In the corridor of United Hospital Center near the pharmacy, there are beautiful paintings of flourishing trees. At the spine clinic, there is a large painting with trees in the background and a big yellow leaf that is changing colors, floating aimlessly in midair, and dominating the painting. The magazines that came in the mail had pages of shrubbery and flowering trees.

The trees, bushes, and leaves made me think about the transitions many of us go through in the various seasons and stages of our lives.

There are many references in the scriptures about trees, and a few about bushes. Psalms 1 tells us about two men, two ways, and two destinies. The blessed man is compared to "A tree planted by the rivers of water, that brings forth its fruit in its season, whose leaf shall not wither; and whatever he does shall prosper." Psalms 92:12 tells us that, "The righteous shall flourish like a palm tree…" In Jeremiah 17, we hear about the man whose heart departs from the Lord, being like a shrub in the desert. Thinking symbolically, how often on this journey of life have you been like a tree—deeply rooted, standing firm, thriving, being blessed, and being a blessing? Can you recall your "bush" days? These would be times when roots were coming detached, and you found yourself wavering, unsteady, unsure, and fertile soil for ungodly things. Then there could be the "leaf" times—times when you were seriously falling, detached from the Word, and blowing aimlessly in the wind.

Personally, I can recall going through all the phases.

Think about your bush times—a time when you may have found yourself lonely, depressed or even in a state of self-pity. Was it because you were out of fellowship with other believers? Was it because you moved away from God and forgot or refused to give Him your forwarding address?

Were those also the times you did not have time to pray, study His word or do daily devotions?

What do you recall about your leaf time—just being out there with no purpose or closeness to God?

How we spend our time and nourish our body, mind, and souls is in direct correlation to whether we stand tall, firm, and flourishing like a tree planted by the river, or a bush shriveling in the desert, or a leaf detached and blowing in the wind.

"Tree" season is the goal and the greatest. There is peace, joy, and comfort in prayer, studying His Word and fellowshipping with other believers. There is hope in being deeply rooted.

If you are in the "bush" or "leaf" stage, just remember, "There is no condemnation in Jesus Christ…" (Romans 8:1). Strive to put old things behind you and be like the "river tree."

Keep in mind that when the praises go up, blessings come down. Be blessed!

# True Colors

$\mathcal{S}$ everal things have happened over the past few weeks that caused me to have flash backs of a game that our family has enjoyed over the years. The game is called "True Colors." At family gatherings, especially during the holidays, it has been a custom for our family to play games in which everyone can participate. One of the favorites has been the game "True Colors." The subtitle of the "True Colors" is "Do you see yourself as others see you?" The teens really enjoy this game because it gives them an opportunity to share their "real" thoughts about some of the adults. The game includes voting cards, question cards, voting boxes and score pads. Each player chooses a color. Then to begin the game, all players— at the same time—pull and *secretly* read their question card. Each player then decides which player (or players) his or her question best describes. Each player must always cast two votes, matching the chosen players' color. The two votes can be two different color-voting cards for two different players or two voting cards of the same color if you feel strongly about that player. Players can also vote for themselves; however, once a voting card is dropped into the box, it stays in box until counted. No changes!

The types of questions are as follows:

- If someone here moved away, you would never hear from this person again. WHO is this?
- You must spend one year on a desert island. You can take one person with you. Whom will you pick?
- If life were like an interstate highway, WHO got off at the wrong exit?

- WHO loves to make silly faces at security cameras in bank lobbies and ATM machines?
- WHO never makes New Year's resolutions—but should?
- WHO could be a licensed back seat driver?

The fun and laughter begin when the questions are read and you realize from the votes, how others see you. While this activity opens communications and allows one to reflect on how others may perceive you, it is all done in fun.

There are life situations that too often parallel this game but are not at all funny.

Death is one of those situations that cause "true colors" to be exhibited. Recently an acquaintance passed, and his biracial children were forced to witness and be subjected to the "true colors" of their father's family. The façade was over, and rejection replaced acceptance. Unfortunately, I have seen this happen too many times. Death seems to allow the often-suppressed ugliness to rear its head. Rejection, disdain, and greed come alive. Why is that?

Friendship can also be dubious. Thinking someone is sincere, caring, and supportive will leave you in a quandary when you learn otherwise. The adage, "If it looks like a duck, quacks like a duck, you better believe that it is a duck," holds true. When someone shows you their "true colors," believe them!

The journey of life provides many opportunities to see bright, beautiful, and vivid colors. Enjoy the "true colors." Do waste time and energy trying to change or camouflage the obvious. Identifying and accepting the "true colors" is like knowing the truth. Moreover, as the scriptures tell us, "The truth will set you free."

The game "True Colors" might be used as an exercise to look beyond your exterior self. Just remember, "Let your light shine before men, that they might see your good deeds…" (Matthew 5:16).

# Try Being Spontaneous

*A*re you stuck in a rigid daily routine? Do you begin your day (after your daily devotions), by making a to-do list? Are you primarily concentrating on paying bills, scheduling chores, completing tasks, scanning Facebook, and checking email? Do you schedule in some fun time or time to connect with friends, relax, and enjoy this precious time allotted to you? Why not?

Do not let life pass you by leaving few pleasant memories for loved ones. Take time to enjoy this life. Take time to smell the roses!

Enhance your days and make fond and pleasant memories with family, loved ones and friends. In other words, seize the moment! Think about how delicious and refreshing it is to have a piece of Dove chocolate slowly melt in your mouth. It is a wonderful sensation! That can be a similar experience when you spontaneously call a friend to go for coffee—or better yet—ice cream. That warm and fuzzy feeling makes for a lasting memory. And it might be one worth repeating.

Be spontaneous and play a board game with the kids or a friend. Scrabble would be great if you can find anyone that will play with you! Enjoy each moment!

"The life of mortals is like grass, they flourish like a flower of the field; the wind blows over it and it is gone, and its place remembers it no more…" (Psalm 103:15–16).

An ancient philosopher Heraclitus once said, "You can never step in the same river twice." As the waters flow, the river constantly changes. Life is always changing around us. Family and friends are leaving us. Nothing stays the same, and we know tomorrow is not promised; however, we can Praise and thank God for today knowing that He never changes. "Jesus is the same yesterday, and today and forever" (Hebrews 13:8).

It is okay for you to be spontaneous sometime! When God said, "Let there be light," the light was spontaneous. The light expresses God's love for us. So if we "trust and depend on Him… He will direct our way" (Proverbs 3:5–6). So being spontaneous is not frivolous. It is living and enjoying the life He has given us.

Prepare a meal and take it to someone living alone, or take it to share with a neighbor, a friend, or a shut in. That is spontaneous!

Call a friend to go see a movie and maybe have dinner. "This is the day the Lord has made; let us rejoice and be glad in it" (Psalm 118:24). You do not have always have to plan things in advance. They can be spontaneous!

It is a blessing to have someone to laugh with, to love, and to enjoy. By being spontaneous, you might be an unexpected blessing to someone. Try it! And you too will be blessed!

# Try This...

*D*uring the seventies, there was a very popular cliché that ran rampant: if it feels good, do it! This saying appeared on posters, postcards, billboards, and was even painted on highway overpasses. Unfortunately, a large percentage of the population took that saying to heart and did just that. Consequently, we began to see a notable increase in moral decline. The number of unwed pregnancies spiraled. Marijuana and heroin use became more and more common. The HIV and AIDS epidemic was upon us. If it feels good, do it, made its impact! And it did not stop there. We are still feeling and suffering from the impact of those who indulged in that philosophy. Many of my friends and classmates that were partakers of that cliché are no longer here with us. Many of you may have knowledge or possibly memories of those days and know of the lives lost and families humiliated and/or destroyed. However, let us move on, and try this.

Whether you are an adamant comfort seeker, or just someone who wants to enjoy the best quality of life possible, try the recommendations listed below. Without a doubt, you will find yourself happier and more content.

When you wake up in the morning, smile and thank God for one more day to do His will! Remember it takes more muscles to frown, so prevent wrinkles. Just smile!

If you live alone, mornings are a perfect time to talk with God. Starting the day with "Here I am, Lord, use me," will not only make for a happy day, but it will also bring you joy! Try it!

If you are fortunate enough to have someone else in your home, be sure to greet them warmly and check on how they rested last night. Their response might be an opportunity to make some changes or accommodations that will make their lives better. It could be something as simple as opening or closing a window, changing the thermostat setting, or installing a night light. Look for an opportunity to show kindness and be helpful. And then do it. Watch and see how much better your day goes and theirs also. Try it!

Start the day's activities with a devotional study, Bible readings, or whatever it takes to connect you with God. Be open and willing to "dig deeper" into His Word daily. Do not just read it, apply it. Make a difference! Try it.

Try some physical exercise. If you are not able to get out and walk or get to a gym, set a timer, and just walk through the house. There are several aerobic exercises that will help strengthen and keep you flexible. Many of these can be done laying down or sitting on a chair. There are programs on TV that you can exercise along with, or you may even want to invest in a DVD exercise series. Exercise makes a big difference. If you are able, do not neglect exercising. Exercising is necessary for your overall well-being. Please try it!

Make plans to do something fun. Set a date and time for an activity that you would enjoy. It might be to see a movie, take a bus trip, or even go shopping. Give yourself something to look forward to doing. If it does not happen, do not get frustrated, reschedule. It gave you something to look forward to and served a purpose. After all, we know things happen. Weather changes and so can plans. Keep thinking ahead and planning. Having something to look forward to gives you a different attitude about life. Try it!

If you want an adventure, or something different in your life, try reading. A good book can provide excitement, take you places you may not be able to afford to travel to, and educate you on almost any topic. Check your local library for best seller lists or check with friends to see what they are reading that might interest you. Reading opens the world to you. Take the opportunity to enjoy a good book and expand your horizons. Try reading!

Look for some way to show compassion or love to someone that needs it. There are so many needy and hurting individuals that just need a kind word, a touch, some token to say that they are worthwhile and that someone cares. Philemon 1:7 says, "Your love has given me much joy and comfort…for your kindness has often refreshed the hearts of God's people." Try to touch someone's heart each day. Remember that each act of kindness that we extend to others, not only nourishes that person, but it also nourishes anyone else within range.

Try this exercise. Make a list of people who have shown you by example how to refresh and help others. Next, make a list of others in your circle of influence who may be refreshed from watching you live out Jesus's love. Are you doing His will?

Above all, try this: PRAYER! When we pray, Heaven responds and is on the scene. While we readily rely on ambulances, EMTs, doctors, and nurses as first responders during emergencies, let us learn to make prayer our first responder (1 Thessalonians 5:17). Try it. You will see and know the difference!

# We Are Defined by Our Choices...

*I*n the play Julius Caesar, Cassius says to Brutus, "Men at some time are masters of their fates: The fault, dear Brutus, is not in the stars, but in ourselves."

That statement implies that we, as individuals, are accountable for our choices, and subsequently for our futures. From our youth, the choices we make affect our lives and shape our futures. The roles we choose during our school years may be that of a jock, prom queen, nerd or geek, or a social butterfly. Whatever the choice, it identifies us, and carries a lasting memory with our classmates, and often throughout our lives. Associating with people of similar interests allows those relationships to help shape our identity. When it comes to choosing a spouse or significant other, another statement is made about our identity!

Taking a quick look at the scriptures, we will find stories of moral choices with significant consequences. Possibly, one of the best known is King David's choice to have an inappropriate sexual relationship with Bathsheba. This indiscretion helped shape his future and result in sad consequences for his children. This is one clear example that our choices do carry consequences.

Looking more recently at American history, former President Bill Clinton had his image tainted by his choice to have inappropriate relations with an intern. Think about the impact this choice had on his wife and daughter and the family of the intern—heartache and humiliation! Notably, we can also recall several sport figures who have significantly scarred their images and hope of future accolades because of allegations of the misuse/abuse of steroids. All these choices paint a negative picture of all involved. In addition to their families having to deal with the stigmas connected to their indiscretions, they, while not intimately connected, also suffer hurt and disappointment in someone they supported and followed. So many are affected by one individual's choice.

Choices—we make them every day. Sometimes we make good choices and sometimes our choices are not the best. Whether good or bad, every choice we make has a consequence. We must always be cognizant of the fact that each decision and choice we make is not affecting only you! The choices we make not only affect our lives, but those choices affect and influence the lives of all those people who love and care about you.

With the abuse of drugs being so prevalent in our community, it is not difficult to see the heart ache caused by those making the choice to sell and provide poison that is killing and depriving so many of having a fruitful life. That "career" choice provides a clear perception of a lack of concern about God's purpose for their life. Moreover, there will be consequences for those actions!

Do not try and blame your choices on others, heritage, culture, or environment. Take responsibility for your choices. Know that bad choices and decisions can be forgiven, and you can move on and become new—2 Corinthians 5:17. Second chances are available. Choose to take them! (Matthew 8:22).

Do not let the world define you. Choose to serve unselfishly and your shining faith and glowing love will define you.

# What Do You See When You Look at Me?

*A* recent article dealing with race issues in *The Oprah Magazine* brought back many memories around this question.

Speaking figuratively, what do you see when you look at me? This question ponders the minds of many people—if they are honest with themselves.

This is not just about color, but all those folks that are noticeably different—folks that are disabled, folks that are obese, folks that are height challenged (short or tall), or those of a different ethnicity.

If you are the only one with a noticeable difference in a homogenous group, are you confronted with stares or even worse, made to feel invisible? While even we Christians claim not to be prejudiced, we too often prejudge. What is the difference between prejudging and being prejudiced?

Being a female person of color, I can share not what I have heard, but what I have personally witnessed. Many of you, I believe, may have had similar experiences.

While attending Indiana University of PA in the sixties, as a college student I could eat in the local restaurants and try on clothing in the department stores, but learned that the local residents of color were not granted the same privileges. Did attending college change one's physical appearance? This was almost unbelievable to me at the time, because growing up seventy miles east of Indiana was a very different experience.

Later in the sixties, when searching for an apartment, all negotiations, including employment verification, were handled over the phone, but when I went to pay the deposit and they saw my face, the apartment was suddenly not available. While extremely frustrating, the blessing was that it led me to become a homeowner!

Then there was the time I drove sixty miles to do classroom presentations at one of the high schools only to be told that there was a change in plans and have the door slammed in my face. I guess I just did not meet that teacher's expectations!

Being a woman of color and the only female in an executive board meeting is an emotionally draining experience I will not even attempt to describe! What an eye-opening learning opportunity. "All that glitter sure ain't gold!"

It is unfortunate and certainly not God's teaching that we seem to take one step forward and two steps back!

Too often we form an opinion about an entire group (nationality, ethnicity, church denomination or social club) based on the actions of one individual. In heaven, there are no ethnic groups, no races, and no distinctions. Why are they so important now?

Dig a little deeper: Read 1 Samuel 16:7, Isaiah 53:2–5, Acts 10:34–35, Colossians 3:5–11, 2 Corinthians 3:18, Galatians 3:26–29.

By the way, look in the mirror. What do you see? Whose reflection is lurking in the background. Pray about, what do you see when you look at me?

# What Else Have I Been Wrong About?

ave you ever had to face the reality that you are absolutely, unequivocally wrong about something or someone? What a slap in the face! And what a reminder to search the scriptures!

Recent events brought this question foremost to mind.

There may have been a time in your life when you studied hard and long for an exam and you were quite sure that you knew the material. On the day of the exam, your confidence was high. You had prepared, studied, and was ready to do it! The essay questions seemed easy enough. You completed the exam, and left the classroom smiling. The next day you find that you misread one of the questions and answered it completely wrong! In haste, not paying close attention to details was costly!

I recall a Statistics class (my least favorite class), when I felt I was definitely prepared for the exam; however, I wasn't prepared for the classroom. This class was held in the auditorium at CMU, and for this exam, the professor changed the seating arrangement. The seat I was moved to was in a somewhat dark area, and there was not enough light for my solar calculator to work. I panicked! My mind went blank! I had to leave the room, regroup, and then get a different seat. With all that happening, I did not have enough time to finish the exam. Knowing the material just was not enough!

Perhaps you have had a neighbor or co-worker that you avoided being near because you felt they were arrogant or snooty. Then one day, you overheard a conversation where this person was praying for others. Taking time to learn a little more about that person, you find they have a deeply spiritual life that includes praying for just about anyone who crosses her path. "Judge not, that ye be not judged" (Matthew 7:1).

Have you ever been shopping for bargains and came home happy with what you thought was a fantastic deal? Then, upon scrutiny, you find you purchased a "knock-off." On the other hand, perhaps, you thought a furniture purchase was solid oak, until you had it in your home and found it to be laminate. Wrong again!

These are small things that may impact one or two persons, but there are much bigger things going on that impact many!

Recent happenings across our country have made it obvious that breaking down racial barriers once again confronts all of us. Yes, I was wrong about something else—thinking that the crumbling walls of prejudice, bigotry, and racism were history. I say crumbling, because the remnants were and will always be visible *in this world*, but I guess it was HOPE that led me to believe that much of that ignorance, hate, and prejudice was in the past. However, once again we are facing full-blown ignorance, prejudice, and bigotry. Whether divisions are racial, political, economic, or educational, the only possibility for reconciliation is through the power and love of Jesus Christ. We must take a swing at these barriers and work for change—each day, each situation, each person at a time—beginning in your own heart and backyard (Matthew 7:1–6, Luke 6:37, John 7:24).

# What Have You Done for Me Lately?

*H*ave you ever had one of those days when you wake up feeling grumpy, depressed, or just lonely? Negative thoughts float through your mind like—what would life be like if I lived in a different place where the weather is warmer? How different would life be if I had a companion/mate? Why am I having this pain? The pity party continues.

You begin to question if God has deserted you. You ask yourself, what has God done for me lately? The truth is you are the culprit! Read Numbers 11:1–11. Do you see any resemblance? What has He done for you lately?

Look around. He woke you up this morning. Apparently, you are in reasonably good health and your mind is sound—because you are thinking and grumbling. You are alive! Make the most of your day.

Put on a gospel CD or tune into a gospel radio station and be thankful that you can hear! Listen closely to the music, and I guarantee you will hear something uplifting, something confirming His presence, or something encouraging you to keep on keeping on.

Pick up your Bible, dust it off, and read Psalm 23. You can see and read. Wow! Who enabled you to see and read? Read the Psalm again. Digest what it says and ponder, what has He done for you lately?

So it is time for breakfast. Do you have food in the house? Who is your provider?

We too often take too many little things for granted. We do not take time to appreciate and be thankful for all the little things He provides daily that makes our time here on earth easier to bear.

Focus on this. Have you done anything lately for someone?

Have you encouraged someone so that sin's deceitfulness does not harden his or her heart? Have you told someone—good job or nice haircut? Have you said something to let someone know they are seen—visible to you and worthy of your attention?

Have you encountered someone with a problem like something you have been through? Did you take the time to share how you were able to overcome and be victorious? Be watchful. Be prayerful. Be ready to share hope, and do not be ashamed to share how He cares for you.

What has He done for you lately? The **Cross** tells it all.

Toss back the negative thoughts and feelings that the enemy is throwing your way and look up. "My grace is sufficient for you, for my power is made perfect in weakness" (2 Corinthians 12:9).

"I have learned to be content whatever the circumstances" (Philippians 4:11).

Share what **He** has done for you lately. You might be pleasantly surprised at the difference it makes. And do not forget to take every opportunity to serve or do something for someone else. After all, it is not just about you!

# What Is in the Box?

At Christmastime, there are boxes of all sizes under the Christmas tree or hidden in various places. Kids of all ages are anxiously waiting to unwrap, open, and hopefully be pleasantly surprised. There is an element of anticipation, anxiousness, and then the SURPRISE!

Christmas excites many of us. We spend time shopping, wrapping gifts, making pretty bows, and doing our best to please and make our loved ones happy. Even if the box is not wrapped in pretty paper, it is welcomed. The gift may be in a stocking. It may be in a gift bag or just have some tissue paper around it. Very seldom do we hear complaints about the wrappings. The gifts are accepted "as is." It is satisfying to see the smiles and hear the giggles as the gifts are opened. The excitement and interest are high even though it is unknown what the box or package contains. We take for granted the box contains something good.

Would it not be great, if we were to have that same attitude about people? Galatians 3:28 confirms, "There is neither Jew nor Greek, slave nor free, male or female, for you are all one in Christ Jesus." There is so much division in our society, often because we look at the packaging a person comes in, and do not take the time or opportunity to check out what is inside. Focus on the character of the heart. Zero in on the uniqueness of the individual. What does it matter if the package is red, yellow, green, black, or white? Fat or thin? Blonde, red hair or brown-haired person? Disabled or buff? If we would spend less time in pointing out differences and more time in focusing on the FACT that Jesus loves all the children of the world, we could make this community and this world a better place.

We must learn to not just accept differences but to value and appreciate differences.

While Christmas is a perfect time to receive, open, and explore a variety of boxes, give some serious thought to the "gift" boxes you encounter daily. Take some time to explore beyond what your eyes see. You owe yourself the opportunity to be blessed by what God has allowed to come into your life. Be open. You might really be pleasantly surprised at what you find. Norman Vincent Peale said, "Change your thoughts and you change the world." The scriptures tell us, "Love one another as I have loved you."

That is my story, and I am sticking to it.

Take time to appreciate not just the box, but what is inside!

# What Is It about a Name?

*N*ames and titles have meaning and when spoken or seen visually, they can paint a picture or give a definite impression.

I was gifted a bookmark personalized with my name. It read "JoAnn - God is Gracious." I Googled the name JoAnn and found that the biblical meaning of the name is God is gracious. Another meaning however, says that Joann is usually a mother of five, with no middle name and is seen as a philosopher to her family, friends, and pet of the house. How about that? Upon hearing the name JoAnn, those in my family and circle of friends may immediately think JoAnn James. There may be that kind of association or connection, but that is only a small group of people. In that group however, you will find many different opinions and thoughts about JoAnn. Other names promise certain guarantees.

Branding, for instance, has created many trademarks that are famous and well known worldwide. In almost every country, you will find a McDonald's. When you see the golden arches or hear that name, the immediate response or associative guarantee is fast food—burgers and fries! Wal-Mart is another example that has worldwide recognition—a variety of products and foods at reasonable prices. In the sports arena, you will see the Nike brand everywhere. Coca-Cola is another name and trademark that is known worldwide.

In the clothing industry and cosmetics field, there are certain brands that have a name that is recognized and respected worldwide.

Names like Michael Jackson, Cher, Beyoncé, Whitney Houston, Celine Dionne, The Temptations, Luther Van Dross, or Jennifer Lopez are world famous and recognized for their talents and trials.

When you hear the word *mother*, what are your thoughts? Could it be, Mother—the one who taught my infant lips to pray, love God's holy word, and walk in wisdom's pleasant way? Mother has a special meaning to each of us.

Some names just trigger certain thoughts. The initial reaction to the name *Rehab* is probably prostitute. Jezebel is known and thought to be a scheming evil woman. Then there is Esther and Ruth—kind and loving individuals. What is it about a name?

Bottom line is that there is only one name that is like no other—Jesus. Jesus—a powerful name that has no rival. His trademark is that He is a provider. He is our strength. He is our help. He is our protector. He is our healer. He is the center of all our joy. He is our all and all. He is the one who redeemed us, and He is the one who will return for us. Read 1 John 4:15, Isaiah 46:4, and Romans 5:2–15. Let the trademark of John 3:16 be forever present in your head and heart and do your part to spread the name of Jesus worldwide.

# What Is Your Stash?

*S*tash is an accumulation of money or perceived valuables that are filling our storehouse. What is in your storehouse? What do you treasure?

Are you at a point in your life where you need to seriously consider downsizing? On the other hand, are there aging or health issues that are forcing you to perhaps, ponder right sizing? Whatever the situation, there comes a time when we must evaluate our "stash."

Surveying your home, do you find that you are guilty of collecting and holding on to items that you no longer use or clothing that no longer fits? Why do you still have these items? Have you simply not had time to purge, or are you leaving all your "stuff" for someone else to have to deal with after you are gone? Think about it!

Many of us are collectors of things that have a sentimental value or things that we find pleasing to look at, or perhaps even things that have potential monetary value—such as certain coins. There is absolutely nothing wrong with that, and some collections can be a healthy, rewarding hobby. Several years ago, I allowed myself to be put on a guilt trip because I was not collecting souvenirs of my travels. Not wanting to add any more clutter to my life or home, I was hard pressed to think of something I wanted to collect. It took much thought and prayer before I found something that I could live with collecting. It had to be something that would not take up a lot of space in either my luggage, or my home. Moreover, it could not be anything expensive! Thimbles now adorn one shelf in the curio! Now when asked, what did you buy on your last trip, my response is a thimble! The guilt is gone, and the thimble collection takes up very little space. Some of the thimbles are useable, but many are just decorative.

The reality television shows about hording and the sad state that these folks are in may make you think about the clutter in your life. You may think, "Thank God, at least I'm not that bad." However, if you are just holding on to things, is there much difference? The programs about hording, and all the books about clutter and how to organize and "declutter" are designed to help us with our "stash." However, it appears it is hard for most of to let go of "things."

Consider this: "Do not store up for yourselves treasures on earth... But store up for yourselves treasures in heaven... For where your treasure is; there your heart will be also" (Matthew 6:19–21).

What is your stash? What is in your storehouse?

# What's Love Got to Do with It?

*I*n 1993, a movie was released entitled *What's Love Got to Do with It?* The movie is the biography of recording star Tina Turner. It reveals how Tina discovers the love of singing from singing in her church choir. However, once she pursues singing as a career, she meets the charismatic Ike Turner, and her life is forever changed.

The movie was a hit, as was the title song, which was composed of the following lyrics:

> You must understand
> Though the touch of your hand
> Makes my pulse react
> That it's only the thrill
> Of boy meeting girl
> Opposites attract
> It's physical
> Only logical
> You must try to ignore
> That it means more than that
>
> (Chorus)
> Oh what's love got to do, got to do with it
> What's love but a secondhand emotion
> What's love got to do, got to do with it
> Who needs a heart?
> When a heart can be broken

It may seem to you
Thant I'm acting confused
When you're close to me
If I tend to look dazed
I've read it someplace
I've got cause to be
There's a name for it
There's a phrase for it
But whatever the reason
You do it for me

(Chorus)
I've been taking on a new direction
But I have to say
I've been thinking about my own protection
It scares me to feel this way

(Chorus)
What's love got to do, to do with it
What's love but a sweet old-fashioned notion
What's love got to do, got to do with it
Who needs a heart when a heart can be broken?

The story portrays Tina falling in love with Ike and enduring years of physical and mental abuse, trying to please him and maintain a musical career. When you look at the lifestyle they were living, the abuse, control, and disrespect, there was confusion and misunderstanding about the true meaning of love.

The dictionary defines *love* as "an intense affection for another person based on familial or personal ties." On the other hand, *lust* is defined as "an overwhelming desire or craving; intense or unrestrained sexual craving." Perhaps you will agree that the Turners had the two words confused!

Just recently, one of the columnists wrote about "A Labor of love" sharing a story of a family that suffered a tragic loss yet found the strength, faith, and fortitude to come together and build a casket for their loved one. That is love!

Love is an action word. Not beating, controlling, and being domineering as Ike was in Tina's life, but just the opposite. "Love is patient; love is kind and envies no one. Love is never boastful, nor conceited, nor rude; never selfish, not quick to take offence. Love keeps no score of wrongs; does not gloat over other men's sins but delights in the truth. There is nothing love cannot face; there is no limit to its faith, its hope, and its endurance. Love will never come to an end."

Who needs a heart? We all do!

What does love to have to do with it? It is all summed up in John 3:16, "For God so loved the world that He gave His one and only Son, that whoever believes in Him shall not perish but have eternal life." That is what love has to do with it!

# When and Where Is Your Reservation?

*T*he dictionary defines *reservation* as "an arrangement by which accommodations are secured in advance," or "the record or promise of an arrangement." At certain times of the year, like Mother's Day, Father's Day, and/or Easter, many folks decide to take advantage of one of the many buffet offerings. To assure accommodations, advance reservation is required. To hold the reservation, the restaurant requires a name, a time, and the number in your party. When that day arrives, you and your party need only to "show up" at the designated hour to enjoy a relaxing, work—free, satisfying meal. Traveling by commercial transit is pretty much the same. It is necessary to book your transportation, and pay, before the reservation is confirmed and the ticket issued. If your travel plans include overnight stay, to assure that you have accommodations, reservations must be made in advance. Planning and scheduling are necessary parts of a reservation. If you decide to take a class or attend a seminar, registration is required so that you have a "place" in that class. In addition, you may also have to pay in advance. Any of the above-mentioned reservations can be, and often are, cancelled, or postponed and rescheduled. Sometimes there is a penalty imposed. Other times, it is just a matter of rearranging plans.

Think about all the things on this journey we call "life," which require a reservation and preplanning. Now, stop and think about the decisions and choices we make daily and how these choices affect and influence that final reservation that has been made for each of us. Death. Death is the one "reservation" that we cannot cancel or postpone. The little dash (–) that is on our tombstone between our birth date and our final "reservation" represents all that we did do, or did not do, to confirm our destination! We may not be able to change the when, but the choices we make do determine the Where. Therefore, I recommend that you live humbly, love deeply, laugh heartily, and pray daily. Our decisions (choices) do determine our destination!

"Commit to the LORD whatever you do,
and your plans will succeed." (Proverbs 16:3).
"The noble man makes noble plans, and by
noble deeds he stands" (Isaiah 32:8).

# When Life Hands You Lemons, Make Lemonade

"When life hands you lemons, make lemonade" is a well-known saying. The meaning of this cliché depends on who you are talking to and the situation. Most often, someone is telling you to "take the bitter with the sweet." Moreover, the bottom line is to either change your attitude, or change how you deal with the situation.

We all know that the lemon is a bitter fruit. To make lemonade, you need some other ingredients—water, sugar, and possibly some ice and a glass or some other container.

When you suffer the loss of a loved one, it is a bitter feeling. If you have not experienced such a loss yet, keep living and it will happen. How you handle and deal with the future after such a loss, depends entirely on whether you just hold onto the lemon or make lemonade. It seems that each milestone in life, whether it is a birthday, an anniversary, a particular holiday, or vacation time, can cause your emotions to be overwhelming. You can allow yourself to become depressed, wallow in self-pity, or you can find comfort and stand on the promise, "I will never leave you, nor forsake you," and make yourself a pitcher of lemonade.

Recently, a friend and I were talking about the loss of her husband. She shared that the date of her twenty-fifth wedding anniversary was approaching. Prior to her husband's death, they had discussed elaborate plans for this milestone. Many would just dwell on their loss and probably just think about, the "what ifs..." Not so with my friend. She has made weekend reservations at their favorite hotel—booking a room overlooking the water, scheduled lunch with some of their "old" friends and bought herself a gold diamond studded ring to commemorate the occasion. This is what they would have done together if he had lived. A positive attitude, friends, pleasant memories, and faith helped her to make a pitcher of lemonade.

"I know what it is to be in need, and I know what it is to have plenty. I have learned the secret of being content in any and every situation" (Philippians 4:12).

# Where Is Your Focus?

*O*nce again, we have all had the opportunity to witness one of the most important celebrated times of the year. Easter!

How do you celebrate the holiday? Do you dye eggs and fill baskets with chocolate bunnies? Do you plan a big family meal with all the family favorites? Do you buy a new outfit and dress-up for the occasion? Or do you simply focus on our Savior and all He did for us?

Growing up, it was a custom to get an Easter basket filled with jellybeans, marshmallow peeps, chocolate bunnies, dyed eggs, etc. In addition, as an added treat we got three or four live "colored peeps"! The little chickens were cute and delightful. However, they usually did not live very long, and when they died it was horrible. The crying and mourning for the loss were unbelievable! We probably should have been put in "timeout" for the actions we displayed when we found the dead chicks in their box. However, that did not happen, and each year we went through the same rituals. The main highlight of Easter, however, was the new clothes! From top to bottom, everything was new—white straw hats, hair-bows, suit or dress, socks with ruffles, patent shoes, and a new spring coat or cape. Thankfully, in the midst of all the commercial stuff, we did learn about Jesus, the Crucifixion, and His Resurrection, but there was no real explanation for the new clothes, the candy, the peeps, etc. As I grew older, I wondered if in the minds of our parents, the new clothes were symbolic of scriptures—thinking/hoping that new on the outside would make us new on the inside. Would all the newness on the outside create a desire in us to be new on the inside? (2 Corinthians 5:17–18 or Psalms 51:10). I have no clue the significance of the live chicks.

All of the fun things—Easter baskets, plastic eggs filled with candy, gathering of family and friends, and even live peeps, are memorable ways to celebrate, but we must also find a way to incorporate a meaningful message and explanation into all that we do. We can place scriptures in the eggs. Magnets with scriptures and encouraging words could be part of the baskets. Teaching that the new clothes on the outside are how God sees us on the inside and in our hearts when we are saved! It is also a perfect time to explain about judging others before we get to know them (Isaiah 11:3, 1 Samuel 16:7). In other words, do not judge a book by its cover! While it may be nice to have new clothes, those who are not dressed so eloquently may have the newness inside also, that God, sees so clearly.

So where is your focus? Are you more concerned with the outside appearance or the inside condition? Stop looking ahead, looking around, or looking back, or worrying about the outside appearance. Look up and do a cleanup job on the inside!

If we would only learn to focus on the real Superhero—Jesus— He will not only accompany us and bring us through all our sufferings, trials, and pains. He will clean up the inside and supply all our needs! Focus on His promises and look up!

# Which Way Do We Go?

*A*s we travel on this journey called life, many opportunities and many challenges find their way to confront us. It seems that if obstacles are not right in front t of us, they are waiting around the corner. These obstacles can either throw us off balance or strengthen our walk with God.

Perhaps aging makes one more sensitive to trial and tribulations, but it seems that there are so many senseless acts of compulsion occurring these days. It is a common occurrence anymore to see a young life snuffed out from drug abuse. Almost daily, there is a news release about severe child neglect, child abuse, animal abuse, and/or elder abuse. Where does it all start and why? Were there warning signals that no one saw, or did we just turn our heads and look the other way? These chronic problems are almost like a pimple that grew into a painful cyst and then turned into a deadly cancer. What starts out as a small thing often escalates into something so huge that several lives are ruined. For example, it has been said—a little marijuana does not hurt, but then it becomes a little crack, a little heroin, and then painfully, death. Then the real hurt begins—for all the survivors!

There is a saying, "First we make our habits; then our habits make us." If the habits are good, productive, and beneficial to society and self, this is all good. On the other hand, the habits, and compulsions we hear and read about daily, in our newspapers are just the opposite. Let us concentrate on forming some good habits, healthy habits, being productive, compassionate and God fearing.

On life's journey—if you live long enough—you will encounter the obstacles of poor health, troubled and/or failed relationships, financial hardship, and some other difficult circumstance. The key is to press on. With God's help and strength, you can and will overcome all obstacles. Believe me. Been there. Done that!

An attitude of gratitude for what you already have and for what God has already brought you through will prepare you for, and help you conquer what is coming next. A "good" habit is focusing on God's goodness and mercy and training our hearts to continue to love God even through the troubling times. God's love does not keep us from trials and troubles but sees us through them and gives you peace. In Joshua 1:5, we find these words: "I will be with you; I will never leave you nor forsake you." Stand on that promise!

You will know which way to go if you "in all thy ways acknowledge Him, and He shall direct thy paths" (Proverbs 3:6).

Tuck this scripture securely away in your heart and there will be no doubt which way to go.

# Who Am I?

Who am I? This is a question, I believe we all could benefit by spending some time in sincere thought and praying about "the real me." Ponder over all the roles you have, and the various relationships intertwined in your life. For example, you might begin with, I am a daughter. I am a sister. I am a mother. I am an aunt. I am a grandmother. I am a friend. I am a chauffeur—transporting kids to various activities, or transporting a spouse or aging relatives to doctors appointments, etc. I am a volunteer, involved in several community organizations, and the list goes on and on. Yet the visual we have of ourselves is not always very positive. Why is that?

Perhaps, asking ourselves some specific questions, and answering them, would improve our self-esteem or help give a clearer picture of who we are. Do you try to comfort and encourage others? Do you share your blessings? Are you available and willing to help those in need? Are you kind and pleasant to others? Are you courteous? Are you truthful and honest? Can your family and friends depend on you when needed? Think about the things that are important to you and rate yourself on where you stand!

Listening to Brian Williams talking about his "downfall" from the anchor spot on national news was a revelation. How easy it is to make "little" mistakes that explode into monstrosities! Trying to make a "false" impression on others, leads to trouble and heart ache.

Think about the images you portray! What do others see when they look at you? What do you want them to see? Are you attempting to hide flaws and shortcomings with designer clothes and designer bags? Do you relish in manipulating others? Are you evasive or forthcoming? Do you lie and embellish your life with exaggerations?

Who am I? It is time for a reality check. Be for real! Come to grips with who you are and deal with it! "Life is fragile. Handle it with prayer!"

And if you are still not sure who you are, look at who God says you are...

Psalm 45:11: Beautiful

Psalm 139:13: Unique

Jeremiah 31:3: Loved

Ephesians 2:10: Special

Jeremiah 29:11: Created for a purpose

Daniel 12:3: Lovely

1 Corinthians 6:20: Precious

1 Peter2:9: Important

Psalm 121:3: Protected

Psalm 103:12: Forgiven

2 Corinthians 5:7: A new creation

Isaiah 43:1: You are Mine!

# Why Do We Do What We Do?

*H*ave you ever had a conversation with yourself about why you do certain things? You would probably be amazed at the answers or reasoning that comes to your mind. We have many missed opportunities to self—evaluate and act. Why do we not do it?

For instance, why do I have a small colorful poster, above the toilet paper, in my guest bathroom that reads, "Wash your Hands"?

You might ask yourself why you do what you do, and if you do not have a justifiable reason, try something else.

Think about these whys…

Why do we send several text messages when one phone call would suffice?

Why do we continue to elect and support politicians who are involved in illicit and/or inappropriate activity?

Why do we continue to bring babies into this world when we are financially and emotionally unable to provide for them or ourselves?

Why do doctors order treatment or refer you to a specialist when there are no appointments available for two to three months?

Why do we subject our bodies to tattoos and piercings when we know the potential for infections, tissue damage, and long-term scarring?

Many of us make New Year resolutions supposedly starting the New Year with plans for needed changes in our lives. At this time of the year, it is usually bitterly cold, snowing and almost everything and everybody is dormant. Most of us are anxiously anticipating and waiting for an end to winter. Why not celebrate Easter with those "New Year resolutions"? After all, His Resurrection brought us new beginnings. The start of spring is like a new beginning. The vegetation is growing, turning green, and new sprouts are forming. The birds are returning from their winter retreat and everything is fresh and anew. Many are even participating in "spring cleaning." It seems to me that Easter would be a very appropriate time for new resolutions. Think about that!

The words of a popular secular song "All of Me," sung by John Legend is so challenging and touching and conveys how our relationship with our Savior should be. Jesus gave all for us, why can't we or do not we give our all to Him?

"The LORD searches every heart and understands every motive behind the thoughts. If you seek Him, He will be found by you; but if you reject Him, He will reject you forever" (1 Chronicles 28:9).

# Why Do We Have Instructions and Labels?

*H*ave you ever purchased a new appliance and refused to read the instructions that came with it and later found that the appliance had many other uses that would have been very useful? If you had only known all the functions of that appliance, you would have gotten so much more use out of it. However, you thought you knew how to use it, so you did not bother to read the instructions.

What about toys? Putting together Christmas toys or even some Christmas trees can be a painstaking adventure. Once again, most of us feel we can handle the project without doing all the reading. After hours of fiddling with the project, we finally get it together, but how much easier it would have been to read the instructions first.

Thank God for the Global Positioning System (GPS) that provides directions to almost anywhere you want to travel. The GPS relieves the burden of asking for directions at gas stations or from local police officers or from whoever may be available. Many of us flatly refuse to ask for directions—even when lost—and have spent many minutes and miles, if not hours, driving aimlessly trying to find our way. Now the GPS takes care of that for us—if we let it!

When sewing, patterns provide essential directions on how to place the pattern pieces on the fabric so that the finished garment will hang properly. Many times, these instructions are ignored, and we wonder why the outfit does not hang properly and looks "home-made." You did not follow the instructions!

When prescribed a new medicine, do you take time to read the warning labels and the small print? Is this being a medication that must be taken with food? Are there certain foods that you should not eat when taking this medicine? What side effects should you watch for? Labels are important! Read them!

Too often, we tend to take instructions and labels too lightly. Just like life. Sometimes we tend to forget that there is a manual for anything we want to do or for any question that we might have. It is called the Bible.

We think we know what we are doing, and we try our best to live a good life, but the thing is Jesus gave us instructions for the best life possible in His Word. Why do we always try to reinvent the wheel when we have access to His illuminating Word?

"Your word is a lamp to my feet and a light for my path" (Psalms 119:105).

Start your day by reading a favorite Scripture or a passage from this manual of love and heed the instructions and warnings in His Word. I believe you will find that these loving warnings will protect and preserve you!

"Do your best to present yourself to God as one approved, a workman who does not need to be ashamed, and who correctly handles the word of truth" (2 Timothy 2:15).

This will also be a help: "I have hidden your Word in my heart that I might not sin against you" (Psalm 119:11).

# Yesterday, Today, and Tomorrow

*A* snapshot view of the world yesterday, today, and tomorrow reveals difficult days and trying times. Folks are tied to their televisions and social media trying to get a clear picture and understanding of the daily impact of COVID-19. People are wondering, is the testing for the virus accurate? Are there people running around with the virus that have not been tested? Are the statistics on deaths and confirmed cases reported accurate? Is stay at home and safe distancing necessary? How long will the safe distancing warning apply?

Then there are those of us needing and wanting salon services—massages, hair care, manicures, and pedicures. When will these facilities be allowed to reopen? Is it possible to "safe distance" for these services?

People are concerned and confused about where to go, when to go, and how to protect themselves. Then there are those who are looking for ways and things to do to help others and be useful during this pandemic. This is a perfect time to use the gifts and talents you have been blessed with. Use your gifts to serve others. Be willing to give, help, and be creative in making the best of this situation. "We are troubled on every side, yet not distressed; we are perplexed, but not in despair; Persecuted, but not forsaken; cast down, but not destroyed" (2 Corinthians 4:8–9).

Although we do not see a physical being, we can feel God's presence touching us, stirring us, affecting our lives, and giving us hope during this uproar of COVID-19. "While we look not at the things which are seen, but at the things which are not seen: for the things which are seen are temporal; but the things which are not seen are eternal" (2 Corinthians 4:18).

We must not let COVID-19 steal our joy. This virus is not something that neither you nor I can control, so we should obey the law of the land and simply turn over all our cares to the experts. I simply say, "God this situation is entirely out of my control. There is nothing I can do to stop or end this chaos, so please take charge of this situation and my life." You will be amazed at the peace that will flood your heart as you turn things over to Him. This does not mean that you are in denial about the virus and the chaos. Instead, you are admitting and committing to the fact that God is enough for your circumstances. When we allow Him to oversee our lives, the battle is already won. We can then understand (Colossians 3:15). "Let the peace of God rule in your hearts…and be thankful for all things."

Regardless of your age, status, gender, ethnicity, you can rely on these words; "Even in your old age and gray hairs, I am He who will sustain you. I have made you and I will carry you; I will sustain you and I will rescue you" (Isaiah 46:4). This is true yesterday, today, and tomorrow. He said it and I believe it!

We are headed for a new "normal." Just let Him be in control of your "normal."

# You Are What You Eat

*I*n the early 1970s, I had the privilege to teach in the program, "You are what you eat."

This was a nutrition education program specifically designed to help families make better food choices, shop, and plan balanced meals on a limited budget. There was also emphasis on weight management and personal images. Eating lots of mashed potatoes, macaroni and cheese, candy, sodas, and breads will often provide what one might call a "plump" look (obesity). On the other hand, eating fruits and veggies might give one a "lean" look. Learning a good balance is the objective. Eat healthy yet be satisfied. Many of the families accepted the teachings. They learned to make meal plans, shopping lists and budget their food dollars. Others seemed to be unable to make any changes. This seems to happen in other areas of our lives also.

Over the years, the "you are what you eat" philosophy has served as a metaphor for me.

While the wrong food choices may cause obesity and other health issues, abuse of different drugs cause other noticeable issues. The meth users commonly have rotten teeth, pocked skin, and sunken eyes. Other drug users suffer malnutrition and are thin and scraggly looking. Others may be jittery and constantly scratching or rubbing their skin as if something is crawling over their bodies. At any rate, there are noticeable signs of discomfort, anxiety, and often-unattractive physical changes. Alcoholics may exhibit signs of slurred speech, stumbling and red eyes. On the other hand, abusers of alcohol or drugs may not have any obvious outward signs—for a while.

Sometimes we tend to blame the choices we make on our environment. While environment is a big factor, our environment is **where we are**, and it is **not who we are or whose we are.** We must recondition our minds to the belief that people do not determine our destiny, God does. Look to the scriptures. Read Psalms 105. Do not settle for mediocrity and get rid of excuses.

Many of us have witnessed parents who teach respect, but then fail to practice that teaching. The children unfortunately model the behavior they see. What they ingest, you see.

Metaphorically, children are a perfect example, of "you are what you eat." The words that come forth from the mouths of children give a good indication of what kind of language they hear in the home. How the child interacts with other children can also serve as a thermometer for what they are seeing at home.

Whether it is food, drugs, alcohol, manners, respect, foul language—what goes in will come out—one way or another. Garbage in, garbage out!

2 Timothy 2:15 tells us, "Do your best to present yourself to God as one approved, a workman who does not need to be ashamed and who correctly handles the word of truth." Read your Bible and fill your mind with His goodness. Think about what goes in your mind, and what goes in your body. Know, "you are what you eat" (ingest)!

In comparison, although most of us do not like to think about mortality, the reality is out of one thousand of us, one thousand will die. You are what you eat!

# About the Author

*J*oAnn, originally from southwestern Pennsylvania, currently resides in NCWV. She attended Hempfield Area Public Schools, Indiana University of PA, Howard University, and subsequently earned a BS degree in social science and home economics from Seton Hill University, and a master's in public management from Carnegie Mellon University. She is a certified facilitator in Performance Management through Development Dimensions International, and a Dale Carnegie graduate. Her professional career spanned more than thirty years in the utility industry, retiring from Hope Gas Dominion Resources and Allegheny Energy.

Actively involved in church most of her life, she is also a graduate of the Pittsburgh Branch of the Moody Bible School and has served as director of Christian education, Sunday school superintendent, presenter of weekly Children's Message, and Christian retreat organizer.

She is currently an active member of Centerbranch Assembly of God, serving as a connect group leader, and maintaining a Prayer Shawl Ministry.

Her past and current volunteer efforts keep her connected to the community, family, and friends. She aspires to give hope, ignite thoughts, and inspire life-changing decisions. She is a loving mother, sister, aunt, cousin, friend, and most importantly a woman of God.

9 781639 613212